SUNNY
DAYS
AHEAD

SUNNY DAYS AHEAD

150 DEVOTIONS FOR HEALTH AND HAPPINESS

LINDSAY A. FRANKLIN

ZONDERVAN

Sunny Days Ahead
Copyright © 2023 by Zondervan

Requests for information should be addressed to:
Zondervan, *Grand Rapids, Michigan 49546*

ISBN 978-0-310-14398-7 (softcover)
ISBN 978-0-310-14406-9 (audio)
ISBN 978-0-310-14405-2 (ebook)

Library of Congress Cataloging-in-Publication Data is available:

https://lccn.loc.gov/2022034850
https://lccn.loc.gov/2022034851

Published in association with the Books & Such Literary Management, 52 Mission Circle, Suite 122, PMB 170, Santa Rosa, California 95409–5370, www.booksandsuch.com.

Zondervan titles may be purchased in bulk for educational, business, fundraising, or sales promotional use. For information, please email SpecialMarkets@Zondervan.com.

Cover Design: Micah Kandros
Interior Design: Denise Froehlich

Printed in the United States of America

23 24 25 26 27 LBC 5 4 3 2 1

INTRODUCTION

This world we live in is dark, difficult, and painful. That's no secret. All you have to do is scroll the news to hear endless reports of death and disease, crime and injustice, cruelty and suffering. On top of the daily struggles we might consider "normal," individuals, nations, and even the entire planet go through times that are extra hard.

Brokenness is part of the package in our sin-fallen world.

So where does that leave us? Helpless? Hopeless? Sometimes it seems that way, and if you've felt those emotions before, you're not alone. Our national mental health crisis proves it, and health experts are particularly concerned about young people's growing fight for mental wellness.

And that's why I'm writing this book. It's for you, friend. Because if you're reading this, I'm guessing you're looking for a better way—searching for tools to cultivate a positive mindset, hoping for reminders of God's unending love, praying for illumination in the darkness.

The truth is, we're not helpless. God breathes hope into his Word. You won't find the words *mental health* or *positive thinking* in Scripture, but you will find examples of perseverance through adversity, reminders of God's faithfulness, and a ton of encouragement for whatever situation you're facing, now or in the future.

You're not helpless, friend. And you're not alone.

WHY THINK POSITIVELY?

The LORD has done it this very day; let us rejoice today and be glad.
PSALM 118:24

It's probably obvious that most people don't want to constantly drown in despair. And if you read your Bible regularly, you've probably noticed encouragements in Scripture to be glad, rejoice, and have a cheerful heart.

But did you know a growing body of research suggests optimism is linked to physical health benefits too? Especially to ward off cardiovascular disease. Isn't that amazing? God's Word encourages us to have a cheerful heart for the sake of our spirits, but positivity is also good for our physical hearts.

Even more encouraging: though this research suggests some people are born more optimistic than others, it also shows optimism can be *learned*. So if we dedicate ourselves to cultivating a positive mindset, we can make real progress in this area. Isn't that empowering?

REFLECTION If you were to rate your current level of optimism on a scale from 1–10, where would you be? By the time we reach the end of this book, where do you hope to be? Write down this goal so you can focus on it as we journey together.

CHOOSING LIFE

This day I call the heavens and the earth as witnesses against you that I have set before you life and death, blessings and curses. Now choose life, so that you and your children may live and that you may love the LORD your God, listen to his voice, and hold fast to him. For the LORD is your life, and he will give you many years in the land he swore to give to your fathers, Abraham, Isaac and Jacob.

DEUTERONOMY 30:19–20

Scripture is full of choices. The choices in this verse—life or death, blessings or curses—were given to the Israelites as they entered the promised land. Through Moses, the Lord told his people they could choose to serve him and receive his many blessings, or they could choose otherwise and reap the bitter consequences.

It can be daunting to think about the consequences we face—including big ones—for bad choices or negative behavior. But it's empowering to think about the fact we *have choices*. A lot happens in our lives that's outside our control, but we always have control of our own behavior. We choose where to focus. We choose how to respond. We can choose life, and that alone is a great gift.

REFLECTION What was the last really good choice you made? Maybe it was small, or maybe it was huge. Either way, how did it feel to choose wisely? Jot down some notes about the experience to remind yourself you are in control of your behavior. You've chosen "life" before, and you can do it again!

DAY 3

SILVER LININGS

When you pass through the waters, I will be with you;
and when you pass through the rivers, they will not
sweep over you. When you walk through the fire, you will
not be burned; the flames will not set you ablaze.

ISAIAH 43:2

You may have been given the advice to find silver linings in bad situations—that is, to try to find the good even when something is bad. But does this work? Is it helpful to add to our positivity tool kit?

It depends, says new research. If the situation is something we can control—for example, getting a bad test grade because we didn't study—finding upsides can be unhealthy, as it kills motivation to change our behavior. Instead of looking on the bright side ("The test didn't count for *too* many points . . ."), a healthier response is changing the behavior that caused the negative circumstance ("I'll make sure to study next time").

But when circumstances are outside our control, looking for silver linings encourages a positive mindset. Finding the good in hard situations helps us pass through the rivers and not be swept under. The fact that the Lord is with us through all our hard times is one huge silver lining! This truth can help us find peace in times of crisis.

REFLECTION Think through a few tough situations you're experiencing now. Are these circumstances inside or outside your control? If they're within your control, what can you do to create change? If they're outside your control, what silver linings can you find?

AFTER GOD'S OWN HEART

I sink in the miry depths, where there is no foothold. I have come into the deep waters; the floods engulf me.

PSALM 69:2

Listen, friend. Before we talk more about tools for your toolbox, choices you control, or looking on the bright side, I want to make sure you understand something really, really important: just because you may struggle with some of these things, that does not necessarily mean there's anything wrong with you or your faith.

We can confidently believe that truth because we have the psalms of David. David wrote the words in Psalm 69, and he wrote many other psalms like it—where he was overwhelmed, downtrodden, searching for God's hand, or praying for intervention. And the Bible says David was a man after God's own heart (1 Samuel 13:14). Wrestling with something does not disqualify us from being a person of faith. It doesn't mean we need to "believe harder" to be accepted by God.

People have been struggling with the issues in our world for millennia. And throughout that time, God has always been there, right beside his people, helping them hold on to their faith in stormy times. This psalm ends on a hopeful, worshipful note. Our struggles can too.

REFLECTION Read all of Psalm 69, noting how David works through his emotions—acknowledging his own sin, pointing out the unfair things happening to him, asking for God's protection, praising God, and looking forward to a hopeful future. See if you can write a journal entry following this model, working through any big, David-sized feelings.

_____

_____

_____

_____

GOD'S PLAN?

"For I know the plans I have for you," declares
the LORD, "plans to prosper you and not to harm
you, plans to give you hope and a future."

JEREMIAH 29:11

One major source of stress as we head toward adulthood is this big, looming question: what is God's plan for my life? Especially when we don't have a clear picture of what the future holds or what we want to pursue. Verses like the one above are often repeated to assure us God has some specific plan for our lives . . . but what is it?

The truth is this verse was written to the nation of Judah while its people were in exile. It was a promise of hope for the future and may be an allusion to the coming Messiah. God's plan for *humanity* has always been specific. Sometimes he also calls individuals to specific things, like when he called Moses (despite Moses's protests) to lead the Israelites out of Egypt.

But if you're not hearing God specifically call you toward something, does it mean there's no plan? There's no need to worry. God has a general plan for each of our lives, and it's really freeing: use your strengths, passions, and skills to share his love with others as you become ever more like Jesus. And over time, he will help guide your future.

REFLECTION Brainstorm lists of your strengths, passions, and skills. Do you notice any themes? What are some plans you could make for your future that involve one or more items from your lists? God made you *you* on purpose. What will you do with it?

SMALL STEPS

Whatever your hand finds to do, do it with all your might.
ECCLESIASTES 9:10

Sometimes it's easy to focus so much on the big plan for our lives that we get overwhelmed, frustrated, and discouraged. Those targets can seem far off—or even unattainable—and it leads to a sense of futility in our daily lives filled with necessary but mundane tasks.

One of the best things we can do when we're hoping to change our mindsets and our lives, as well as reach some big targets, is set small goals for ourselves. Why? Small goals help us build momentum. They help us make tangible progress toward larger goals.

Have you ever known someone who writes items on a to-do list, even though they've already done them, just to be able to check them off? It sounds crazy, but it's true that even the *perception* of progress actually helps us make progress. It's all about momentum. Those small goals you achieve are propelling you forward.

REFLECTION Brainstorm one or two small goals you can set for the upcoming week and track your progress as you work on them. Bonus points if these small goals (such as putting some money into savings) will help you achieve a larger, long-term goal (buying that big-ticket item you've been wanting).

DAY 7

A REASON TO CELEBRATE

There is a time for everything, and a season for every activity
under the heavens: . . . a time to mourn and a time to dance.
ECCLESIASTES 3:1, 4

Ecclesiastes 3:1–8 is an interesting passage, as it highlights such a wide breadth of human experience. Mourning and celebrating, weeping and joy, birth and death. While we might prefer to avoid the darker or more painful experiences that are listed, it's inspiring to receive an encouragement to fully embrace times of joy, life, hope, and celebration.

When was the last time you really celebrated? You don't need a special occasion or holiday in order to celebrate. Small wins deserve recognition. In fact, meeting small goals gives us a perfect reason to rejoice. Whatever area of life we're trying to progress in—our walks with God, our educations, our careers, our mental health, our relationships—positive steps forward merit a positive response.

So throw yourself a little party! Celebration and rejoicing are good for our hearts, and it reinforces our desire to continue meeting our small goals.

REFLECTION Have you had any wins lately, big or small? If so, how can you celebrate them? It can be anything you want, including allowing yourself to rest and do nothing—without feeling guilty! If you haven't had a recent win, set a small goal for yourself right now. And think about how you'll celebrate when you crush that goal.

ROLE MODELS: DAVID

David said to Michal, ". . . I will celebrate before the LORD.
I will become even more undignified than this."

2 SAMUEL 6:21–22

David is such an interesting man to study. He had his issues, and the Bible records several of his worst mistakes, but we also know he had a special relationship with the Lord. He's a role model for us to follow in so many ways. One of these is how he unabashedly, unashamedly danced before the Lord with all his might (2 Samuel 6:14).

David's wife Michal did not appreciate the way her husband was behaving. She accused him of worshiping in a way that was improper for a king. But David was usually more concerned about pleasing God than worrying what others might think of him, and he told Michal so.

We don't need to worship politely. Practice lifting your full voice, your full praise, your full heart to God. Dance if you feel like it. Our joy is pleasing to God!

REFLECTION Have you ever engaged in "undignified" worship and celebration like David? Even if it's not your style to get loud in your celebrations, what's one way you can let go in your praise? Try journaling your praise with no embarrassment, writing like only you and the Lord will ever read it.

GOD'S PROMISES: APPROACH THE THRONE

Let us then approach God's throne of grace with confidence, so that we may receive mercy and find grace to help us in our time of need.

HEBREWS 4:16

God made a ton of encouraging promises that are recorded in Scripture. Some of them are to specific individuals, others are to the tribes of Israel. Others are for us, followers of Jesus living today.

One such promise for us is that we can approach the throne of God with confidence—with boldness, freedom, and openness. If you know how the Israelites approached God's presence in the Old Testament, you'll realize how amazing this promise is. The Most Holy Place was the part of the tabernacle (and later the temple) where God's presence appeared. Only the High Priest was allowed to enter there, and only once per year, on the Day of Atonement.

When Jesus died on the cross, he broke down those barriers between humankind and God. A relationship with God's Son gives us the ability to confidently approach God's throne of grace with boldness and honesty, imperfect though we are. What an incredible gift!

REFLECTION What would you say to God right now if you could enter his presence with freedom and honesty? Guess what? You can! Think of a few things you'd like to say to him today. If it's too tender or personal to write down, that's okay. God hears you.

DAY 10

BUILDING CONFIDENCE

For the LORD will be at your side and will
keep your foot from being snared.

PROVERBS 3:26

D o you ever feel like you're standing in your own way? Cutting your-self off from opportunities, saying no to a dream or goal before anyone else shoots you down? Being overly critical of your own efforts so that nothing feels good enough? These kinds of negative thoughts are called self-rejection, and it's a very limiting mindset, one that can make us feel trapped and helpless.

Setting small goals for ourselves is a great way to break these neg-ative thought patterns. When you set a small, concrete goal and then achieve it, you are training yourself to recognize, yes, you *can* do it. These little wins build confidence over time, and suddenly we're more willing to put ourselves out there. While we are not promised success in everything we do (and failing can be important to build resilience and humility), we are promised that God will be with us as we walk through life, growing us into the people he created us to be.

REFLECTION How did you do on the small goal you set a few days ago? If you haven't reached it yet, don't worry. There's no time limit. Just keep taking steps toward the finish line, and you'll get there. (And when you do, don't forget to celebrate!) Take some time now to think about how you can focus on your progress and encourage any thoughts of self-rejection to take a hike.

DAY 11

TRANSFORMATION

And we all, who with unveiled faces contemplate the Lord's glory, are being transformed into his image with ever-increasing glory, which comes from the Lord, who is the Spirit.

2 CORINTHIANS 3:18

The idea of being "transformed" sounds rather mystical. And in a way, it is. God works on us day by day, giving us opportunities to be shaped and refined into the image of Jesus. Sometimes we call this spiritual growth or sanctification, which sounds supernatural. But the process of being transformed—that is, being changed—is actually pretty practical, even when we're talking about spiritual growth.

It usually consists of daily choices and everyday behaviors evolving over time. We might make big leaps forward sometimes—like the moment we first come to know Christ, or some other pivotal event in our Christian walk. But most transformation happens in quieter, smaller moments over the course of our entire lives.

All these small goals we've been thinking about and working toward can transform us too. Even the champion procrastinator (that's me) can become a productive professional who meets deadlines and teaches workshops on time management.

REFLECTION What's an area of your life where you'd like to be transformed? It can be something related to spiritual growth, like having a closer prayer relationship with God. Or maybe it's something completely practical, like staying better hydrated (hey, it's important). Write down your goal, then write down the specific steps you'll take to get there.

GOD'S PROMISES: ALL THIS

I can do all this through him who gives me strength.

PHILIPPIANS 4:13

You've probably seen this verse before. It's one of the most popular from the New Testament, and rightly so. It's a great, encouraging verse. Sadly, it's often pulled out of context, so we might misunderstand what it's actually saying. The "this" Paul is referring to is what he mentioned in the previous verse—he has learned to be content in all circumstances, whether hungry or fed. He can endure all circumstances through God's strength.

It might seem discouraging to realize this verse isn't a blanket promise that God will empower us to do whatever we want. But when we look closer, this promise is something far more valuable. We know hard times will come—they do for everyone—and Paul's words remind us that the Lord supports us through those hard times. Our joy does not have to depend upon our circumstances. We can endure all this through him who gives us strength.

REFLECTION How does it make you feel to know that whatever circumstances you face, God will help you walk through them? Can you recall a time in the past when you've felt that strength from God, whether it was a great time or a difficult time? Write it down to remind yourself of this promise.

WE NEED ROLE MODELS

Remember your leaders, who spoke the word of God to you.
Consider the outcome of their way of life and imitate their faith.
HEBREWS 13:7

It doesn't matter how old you are, you need good role models. We all do. We need people we can look up to who know more about a subject than we do, who have already achieved something we hope to accomplish, who exhibit good character traits we'd like to emulate.

The Bible is full of wonderful examples for us (as well as some questionable behavior we'd definitely like to avoid). We've taken a look at one role model already—David, who praised God without shame—and we'll look at many more before the end of our journey together, each with something unique to teach us.

Role models we encounter in our daily lives are important too. They motivate us to achieve our goals, try new things, and grow in many areas of our lives. They show us how to live with faith, compassion, integrity, and hope.

REFLECTION List some of your role models, whether they're people you personally know, current or historical figures, or people from the Bible. What do each of those people teach you? What characteristic of theirs do you hope to emulate? See if you can add to this list before you finish this book.

_____

_____

_____

_____

_____

_____

DAY 14

A NEW SKILL

Let the wise listen and add to their learning,
and let the discerning get guidance.
PROVERBS 1:5

Maybe it seems intuitive that learning new skills is a good thing. But did you know studies have linked learning new skills to increased happiness? Scientists theorize that expanding our skillsets increases brain development and flexibility. New skills broaden our perspectives and keep us from falling into ruts.

Perhaps the new skills you want to learn are very practical. It's important to learn essential life skills, like doing the laundry, cooking for yourself, managing money, or navigating roadways. But new skills can also be creative. Learning the basics of photography, how to paint, or how to make your own soap are just a few examples. How about learning to code, writing a novel, or taking up video editing? The possibilities are endless, and not only are these activities fun and brain-boosting, they could also uncover new interests for you or fields you might consider for your career.

REFLECTION Write down two or three practical, essential skills you'd like to learn. Think about what you'll need to know when you're living on your own. Now write down one or more creative skills you'd like to learn. It's easier than ever to find good tutorials online, so don't limit yourself. Take up gardening, learn a new language, uncover the secrets of baking bread. Get curious!

DAY 15

DREAMING BIG

*There is surely a future hope for you, and
your hope will not be cut off.*

PROVERBS 23:18

We've talked about small goals to make quick, tangible progress and help us move forward. But what about long-term goals? Dreaming about the future is really important when cultivating an optimistic mindset. Big dreams remind us that our present situation isn't permanent. There's always something to shoot for, somewhere else to go, a greater purpose to pursue. Dreaming about the future combats feelings of hopelessness and boredom.

We can dream about any area of our lives we want to—creative pursuits, family, career, ministry, travel. We will look at some of these later in this book, but dreaming is the time to let your imagination take off. Maybe you dream of starting a small business, obtaining a certain degree, solving a big problem, impacting your local community in a meaningful way. There's no end to the possibilities you can dream for your future.

REFLECTION Even if all our dreams don't materialize exactly how we planned, the act of dreaming in itself is healthy. Sometimes pursuing those goals leads us places we never imagined. Write down some of your dreams for your future. It'll be fun to return to your thoughts ten years from now to see how things played out.

GOD'S PROMISES: SPIRIT OF POWER

*For the Spirit God gave us does not make us timid,
but gives us power, love and self-discipline.*

2 TIMOTHY 1:7

Sometimes we think of bravery as thrill-seeking. That a brave person is someone who dives off cliffs for fun or can't get enough roller coasters or is an extreme sports junkie. And those things are pretty daring. But when we look closer at this verse, we see a different, perhaps quieter type of bravery—the type God promises to us.

Our God-promised bravery isn't about chasing adrenaline or being known as a fearless person. Our bravery comes from the Holy Spirit, who gives us power, love, and self-discipline. This type of bravery allows us to passionately pursue our faith (as Paul was encouraging Timothy to do), to put aside the cares of this world in order to better love our neighbors. To focus less on what other people think of us and more on what's pleasing to God.

That's the kind of bravery we're promised. No cliff-diving required.

REFLECTION Do you feel you've embraced your God-given bravery? If so, jot down a few times you know God has empowered you to be bold in your faith. If you haven't fully embraced this promise yet, write out a prayer to God, asking him to empower you in love and self-discipline.

DAY 17

BIG DREAMS: EDUCATION

The heart of the discerning acquires knowledge,
for the ears of the wise seek it out.

PROVERBS 18:15

When it comes to seeking knowledge, we live in a fascinating age. In fact, this era is often referred to as the Information Age, because the internet has placed nearly the full breadth of human knowledge at everyone's fingertips. If you want to learn about something—anything—the information is out there for the taking, if you look in the right places (just always vet your sources).

Being a lifelong learner is important for brain health, but what about our more formal educational goals—the education that's likely to lead to our future careers? Is there a degree you want, vocational training you'd love to have, or a particular college you've imagined attending? Maybe instead you've dreamed of a particular career you'd like to have. You can work backward from that goal to determine what type of education will be necessary to achieve your career goal.

REFLECTION Brainstorm a list of ten things you'd love to learn about in your lifetime. They could be related to your future career or classes you want to take through a school—or not. Just think of ten things that truly fascinate and inspire you and write them down.

BIG DREAMS: PARENTHOOD

Children are a heritage from the LORD, offspring
a reward from him. Like arrows in the hands of a
warrior are children born in one's youth.

PSALM 127:3–4

Okay, I know. Thinking about becoming a parent when you're still legally considered a kid might seem crazy. But remember, the act of dreaming about the future is, in itself, healthy. And having kids is a big, giant life decision that could greatly impact your future.

So, what do you think? Have you always wanted to be a parent? To have kids and watch them grow, nurturing and raising them? Or does this sound terrifying to you? Maybe it's a little of both. The Bible tells us children are a blessing, but that doesn't mean children are in everyone's future. Sometimes this decision is within our control, and sometimes it's not. But if it *were* in your control, what thoughts do you have about parenthood?

Parenthood is a crazy-daunting task. A huge responsibility. But it can also be a journey well worth taking. If parenthood seems completely unappealing to you, think of some alternative ways to pour into the lives of others—such as mentoring or volunteering with community outreach programs.

REFLECTION Do you have any experience with kids? Babysitting, hanging out with younger siblings, or working in your church nursery or Sunday school? Has it made you think about having your own children someday? Write out some desires for your future, whether they involve kids or not.

GOD'S PROMISES: NOT BLOTTED

The one who is victorious will, like them, be dressed in white. I will
never blot out the name of that person from the book of life, but
will acknowledge that name before my Father and his angels.

REVELATION 3:5

If you have put your faith in Jesus Christ as your savior, your name is in
the book of life. And the one who is victorious (that's you) will never
be blotted out (erased) from that book. Jesus says here in Revelation that
he will acknowledge our names before his Father.

Wow. That's an awesome promise. We must really hold the awe-
someness of this close—the deep reassurance, but also the weight of it.
Our names are in *the book of life*, never to be erased, and we must live
like it—faithful to our confession, following in the footsteps of Jesus to
the best of our ability. This promise is certainly not a free pass to behave
recklessly, since we can't ever be blotted out. Rather, it's a weighty,
powerful reminder of what an immense blessing we have received,
through no merit of our own.

REFLECTION What emotions come to the surface as you consider the
powerful blessing from God that you, the victorious one who has held fast to
their faith, will not be blotted out from the book of life? Spend a few moments
journaling about what you feel.

_____

_____

_____

_____

_____

_____

MONEY MATTERS

Dishonest money dwindles away, but whoever
gathers money little by little makes it grow.
PROVERBS 13:11

We live in a society—in a world—that's pretty obsessed with wealth. The economy is always at the top of the list of questions presidential candidates are asked about. We are culturally fascinated with people who have lots of money, and you can read articles or watch documentaries about their lives, their possessions, their opinions. It's pretty weird, honestly.

So how do we, as followers of Jesus, engage with money in a healthy way when our society is obsessed with it and the Bible repeatedly warns us repeatedly not to love money? Thankfully, Scripture gives us specific guidance about this. And through that specific guidance, we know it's not money itself that is harmful but instead how people cling to wealth—how they will ignore the suffering of others, engage in dishonest practices, or even directly harm others for money.

The two words that come to mind when summing up the Bible's advice about managing money wisely are responsibility and generosity. These can be our guiding principles as we think about our present and future finances.

REFLECTION No matter how large or small the amount of money you've had opportunity to manage so far (or that you might manage in the future), engaging with it wisely is key. Have you demonstrated responsibility and generosity in the past? How can you continue to do so in the future?

GOD'S PROMISES: HIS CHILDREN

Yet to all who did receive him, to those who believed in his name, he gave the right to become children of God.

JOHN 1:12

In the Old Testament, inheritance was a very important concept. When the Lord gave a specific area of land to the Israelites, he drew distinct boundaries for each tribe of Israel. They had an allotment—an inheritance—set aside especially for them, and this inheritance marked them as God's people. His children. His chosen ones.

When we consider the weight of that Old Testament context, it brings new understanding to this New Testament promise—that those who receive Jesus are given the right to become children of God. This is something deeper than the general truth that everyone is loved by God and created in his image (still an awesome truth in itself). This is marking us as heirs—coheirs with Christ (Romans 8:17). Simply put, we are adopted into the greatest of all families. God is our Father, and we are children who will inherit the promises of his kingdom.

REFLECTION Imagine what it means to be adopted into God's family. We know our inheritance in God has nothing to do with material possessions or wealth—it's a heavenly inheritance. It's hard to even wrap our minds around what that means! But we do know what it means to be a son or daughter. Journal some thoughts about being a son or daughter of God.

ROLE MODELS: RUTH

Ruth replied, "Don't urge me to leave you or to turn back from you. Where you go I will go, and where you stay I will stay. Your people will be my people and your God my God."

RUTH 1:16

Ruth is a fantastic role model for us in many ways. She was faithful, bold, and determined. But one of my favorite things about Ruth is what she represents for all of us. Ruth was not born an Israelite. She married a man who had fled Judah with his parents and brother during a famine. They went to Moab, where Ruth was from, and Moabites were historically the enemies of Israel.

But Ruth didn't let that stop her from chasing after God and community with his people. After Ruth's husband died, she begged her mother-in-law to allow her to accompany her back to Judah, and her request was granted. And once she arrived in Judah, she continued to persevere even when she and her mother-in-law were faced with challenges. Ruth was regarded as a righteous woman and, as the great-grandmother of King David, is part of Jesus's lineage. She was willing to leave behind everything she knew to follow the one true God and be counted among his people.

REFLECTION What are some ways you can follow Ruth's example by chasing after God and community with God's people? Are you regularly attending church, youth group, or Bible study? Is there an online community of fellow believers you could join? Brainstorm ideas and pick one to pursue boldly.

CARRYING OTHERS' BURDENS

*Carry each other's burdens, and in this way
you will fulfill the law of Christ.*

GALATIANS 6:2

We're going to spend a little time focusing on two important principles that must be held in balance—serving others and refilling your cup. There's no question that Scripture tells us we are to serve others. But what does that mean?

In our society, it's easy to adopt a me-first attitude. You might have heard the phrase "looking out for number one." That means putting yourself above all else—doing what's right for you without regard for others, because if you don't look out for you, no one else will. We can say definitively this idea is not supported by Scripture, no matter how much our culture has embraced or normalized it.

There are lots of things that fall into the category of serving others: Looking out for other people. Considering the impact your actions have on others. Living carefully and thoughtfully. Caring about other people's experiences. No matter how we do it, it's important to help carry each other's burdens and show love for our fellow humans.

REFLECTION Is there an area in life where you've adopted a me-first attitude? Are you simply maintaining healthy boundaries, or have you accidentally embraced a selfish mindset? List some ways you can serve other people this week, then go out and do them!

TIME FOR REST

> Then, because so many people were coming and going that
> they did not even have a chance to eat, he said to them, "Come
> with me by yourselves to a quiet place and get some rest."
>
> **MARK 6:31**

Even Jesus got tired. John 4:6 tells us directly, but we can guess he must have been worn out other times as well. He was fully human, and human bodies need rest. We must sleep. But it's encouraging to realize that, though he lived a life that perfectly embraced serving others, Jesus got weary. Sometimes the crowds were overwhelming. The demands were too much.

And when they were, Jesus retreated to quiet places—sometimes with his disciples, sometimes with his very best friends, and sometimes alone—to get some rest. To pray. To recharge. To sleep. These are healthy, important things to do. It's impossible to serve and serve and serve without recharging. And yet many times we try to do just this, and it leads to stress and burnout.

Make time for guilt-free rest. It's healthy, and Jesus modeled it for us. The work of serving others will never be totally complete, and allowing ourselves to rest will enable us to give our best selves to those we serve.

REFLECTION Are you good about making time for rest? What are your favorite ways to recharge? Do you prefer to be alone or surrounded by friends and family? Schedule some time for rest in the coming week and see if having time dedicated to recharging boosts your mood and energy.

DAY 25

MEETING PHYSICAL NEEDS

Whoever is kind to the poor lends to the LORD, and
he will reward them for what they have done.

PROVERBS 19:17

One area of service that is repeated in Scripture over and over again is looking after the needs of the poor. The New Testament repeatedly reminds believers to care for the poor. Does this simply mean in a spiritual or emotional sense? Well, that's part of it. But it's important for us to consider the physical needs of those struggling to get by as well.

Why? Because Jesus did. He healed the sick, fed the hungry, gave sight to the blind. He took note of the physical needs of others, and he often met them, while also sharing his teachings about the kingdom of heaven. The Bible doesn't give us a pass on this. It is absolutely clear that we are supposed to share with those who are in need.

Sharing isn't always about giving money, though that's a great way to help others. You can volunteer your time. You can collect donations. You can raise awareness. You can start small or start big—what's important is that you start!

REFLECTION Brainstorm a list of ways you can use your resources to help others. Do you want to join an organization that already exists? Perhaps start your own? Or maybe there's an individual you'd like to help. Get specific, and get moving.

TIME FOR REFLECTION

Immediately Jesus made the disciples get into the
boat and go on ahead of him to the other side, while he
dismissed the crowd. After he had dismissed them, he
went up on a mountainside by himself to pray.

MATTHEW 14:22–23

Our world is incredibly busy. There's a deluge of information, stimulation, and expectation. It's not only possible but *easy* to stay occupied nearly all the time, whether with work, school, or entertainment.

But Jesus modeled a very important type of personal renewal for us to practice: reflection. He would periodically move away from the large crowds that followed him throughout his ministry travels and retreat to quiet places. Sometimes he would rest, but often he would use the time to pray and reflect. In secluded spaces, he could allow his mind the quietness it needed. The quietness we need.

It doesn't have to be literally silent for you to create a peaceful, open space for your mind to breathe and turn toward God in prayer. Maybe you like to listen to music during these times or be in a location where you can hear nature. The point is to find a peaceful space to give your brain a break from the static of regular life.

REFLECTION   What things do you prefer to have for quiet reflection? Do you like to read your Bible? Light a candle? Curl up under a blanket? If you haven't tried reflection before, experiment and see what works for you.

YOUR BLESSINGS BLESS OTHERS

Serve one another humbly in love.

GALATIANS 5:13

We already talked about the importance of meeting others' physical needs and continuing to "remember the poor," as the Bible states it (Galatians 2:10). But what about other ways we can use our blessings to bless others?

Has God gifted you with a particular talent or skill? Maybe you're an amazing pianist, or are good at building things, or are a very organized person who is great at tracking details. All of these gifts and talents can be used to serve others. Musicians can volunteer their talent at church and other community groups. Builders can help humanitarian housing organizations. Detail-oriented people are always appreciated for administrative tasks (just ask your church secretary).

Maybe you feel like your biggest talent is energy and the willingness to dive in. That's an *incredibly* valuable gift! Ask anyone who has ever run a ministry. No matter who you are, you have been blessed with something to share.

REFLECTION Brainstorm a list of talents or skills you have. Pick your top one or two, then think of a few ways you can share that blessing with others. If you get stuck, you can ask your parents or a leader in your church or community if there are any volunteer or service needs. See if there's something that fits you!

LITERARY THERAPY

Jesus did many other things as well. If every one of them
were written down, I suppose that even the whole world
would not have room for the books that would be written.

JOHN 21:25

I f you're a book nerd like me, the idea of the whole world being filled
with books is actually pretty appealing. Wouldn't it be great if every
one of Jesus's deeds was written down? I would read those books!

If you've gotten this far, you probably like to read—at least a little.
Do you like nonfiction books like this one, fictional tales, or both?

Reading is a great way to refill after you've been pouring yourself
out in service to others. Fictional stories can captivate our imaginations. Nonfiction books can instruct, enlighten, uplift, amuse—or all of
the above. Is there a particular genre you love? A particular type of book
that makes you feel recharged when you read it? That's an excellent
"input" activity—something that refills us. Remember, it's important to
balance input activities with "output" activities—those where we focus
on filling others.

REFLECTION   What was the last really great book you read? What did you
love about it? Try to find three to five similar titles to add to your list of books
to read. Book nerd extra credit: use a book tracker to record your thoughts
about each book.

DAY 29

GENEROSITY

"In everything I did, I showed you that by this kind of hard work we must help the weak, remembering the words the Lord Jesus himself said: 'It is more blessed to give than to receive.'"

ACTS 20:35

The concept of generosity is laced through Scripture, especially the New Testament. "God loves a cheerful giver" (2 Corinthians 9:7). "Give, and it will be given to you" (Luke 6:38). For some, giving comes really easily. They are, by nature, generous people, or perhaps giving is their spiritual gift. For others, this is a real challenge—an area where God's directives challenge and stretch them, pushing them well outside their comfort zones.

Maybe a lot of us are smack in the middle.

But no matter how easy or difficult it comes for us, the challenge is the same—give to others with an open hand and a generous heart. Give, not *only* because it's commanded, though that's a good place to start. Give because it makes your heart glad to do it. Give because blessing someone else brings joy—to you and them.

REFLECTION Would you consider yourself a cheerful giver or a reluctant contributor? If you fall on the reluctance side of the scale right now, that's okay. This is something you can work on intentionally. If generosity comes easily to you already, awesome! No matter which way you lean, what is one way you can generously bless someone today?

REFILLING WITH MUSIC

Let the message of Christ dwell among you richly as you teach and admonish one another with all wisdom through psalms, hymns, and songs from the Spirit, singing to God with gratitude in your hearts.

COLOSSIANS 3:16

Music is another wonderful form of "input" when we're looking to recharge. Music lifts the soul, especially when the music is written to glorify God. While there's nothing wrong with entertainment—music, books, movies—that we enjoy simply because they're fun, there's something special about art created specifically to glorify God.

This is particularly apparent in music. Some hymns have endured for centuries and are still sung every Sunday in churches throughout the world. The words of psalms written millennia ago are still used in contemporary worship songs. It's pretty incredible, when you think about it! Imagine how many millions of people have said or sung those exact words through the ages. It brings to mind a picture of all God's children praising him together, with one voice.

REFLECTION Do you have a favorite hymn or song you sing in church? What do you love about it? Consider trying to build a playlist around that song to find more soul-lifting music you enjoy.

GOSPEL DEEDS

In the same way, let your light shine before others, that they may see your good deeds and glorify your Father in heaven.

MATTHEW 5:16

We know our good deeds don't save us. The Bible is clear that our salvation is based on Jesus's work, not our own (thank goodness). And yet we are still directed to do good things, to work hard, to let our lights shine. Why?

These words of Jesus, recorded in Matthew, point us toward one major reason. When we serve others, we are living out the gospel before their very eyes. We are like representatives for Jesus, showing them what love for humanity looks like. We are acting as a shadowed reflection of God's love for humanity.

Think about that for a moment—you can share the love of Christ with another person without even opening your mouth. By all means, share the good news with words too! But don't forget that your actions send a powerful message to those you serve, one that could spark the faith of others.

REFLECTION Think back on some of the ideas to serve others that you came up with earlier. What's the one idea that resonates for you most? Write down that idea, then brainstorm three practical steps you can take to make progress on that service idea.

ROLE MODELS: MARY OF BETHANY

Then Mary took about a pint of pure nard, an expensive perfume;
she poured it on Jesus' feet and wiped his feet with her hair.
[...] But one of his disciples, Judas Iscariot, who was later to
betray him, objected, "Why wasn't this perfume sold and the
money given to the poor? It was worth a year's wages."

JOHN 12:3–5

When we read this story about Mary (the sister of Martha and Lazarus, not to be confused with other New Testament Marys), our knowledge of Judas helps us frame what's going on. We know he will soon betray Jesus, and that his motives are not honorable.

But Mary didn't know. Judas was a disciple, someone close to Jesus, and a man in a culture where women had little voice. The balance of power tipped in his direction. What did Mary think when he scolded her? Did she get embarrassed? Wonder if she'd done something wrong? The Bible doesn't say, but based on what we know of Mary, my guess is she ignored him. I think Mary seemed comfortable doing what she knew God called her to, even if others didn't understand.

Sometimes God asks us to serve in ways others don't understand. We may face harsh words, even though we know we're being obedient to the Lord. We can look to Mary as an example of how to persevere.

REFLECTION Have you faced unfair criticism about the way you're serving God? Are you able to shake it off? Think through ways you could bring a little Mary into your response next time, reminding yourself of God's promises, or use the space below to draft a ready (but kind) answer.

WAGING WAR

So do not fear, for I am with you; do not be dismayed,
for I am your God. I will strengthen you and help you;
I will uphold you with my righteous right hand.

ISAIAH 41:10

There's a saying that's become popular in recent years: it's okay to not be okay. It's an important idea. The point is to try to remove stigma surrounding mental health struggles. For a long time, it wasn't socially acceptable to admit you were dealing with anxiety or depression, but that's starting to change. It's okay to not be okay.

But it's important to balance this idea with another truth: mental health conditions are treatable. Similar to how we address physical health conditions, we can address mental health conditions in various beneficial ways. We're going to talk about anxiety specifically, filling our toolboxes with practical helps to combat anxious thoughts—but friend, remember that there is relief and support for mental health conditions. If you're suffering, talk to someone: a parent, a trusted pastor or youth leader, a mentor or teacher, or a licensed counselor. If you ever feel like you're losing the battle for your mental health, *reach out*. And also remember, God strengthens and upholds us, even through our darkest times. You are never alone.

REFLECTION Have you ever felt like you're waging a war for your mental health? There are a lot of people in those trenches beside you. Perhaps you don't struggle with this but someone close to you does. Let's say a prayer right now, either for yourself or for those struggling with mental illness around you.

CAPTIVE THOUGHTS

We demolish arguments and every pretension that sets itself up against the knowledge of God, and we take captive every thought to make it obedient to Christ.

2 CORINTHIANS 10:5

For those battling anxiety, thoughts probably don't feel much like obedient, well-trained puppies. More like deranged gophers gnawing through our sense of peace and security, or an angry nest full of irritated hornets. Or even a crash of emotional rhinoceroses, ready to trample us at any moment. And yet Paul says here we *can* take captive every thought and make it obedient to Christ.

Rather than become frustrated that we fail to do this perfectly, let's think of this verse as empowering. We may not be able to completely control our anxious thoughts, but we do have a choice over what we'll do with those thoughts. Will we allow them to force us into a spiral, diving face-first into the hornets' nest? Or will we refuse to listen to the lies the enemy—and sometimes our own brains—try to feed us? We have the power to choose which thoughts we embrace and which we reject, and we have the power to embrace the truth that God loves us. *Always.*

REFLECTION   In the space below, try this exercise. Visualize your anxious thoughts as some sort of creature—a deranged gopher, for example. Imagine capturing that gopher in a cage where he can't hurt you (or himself, poor thing). You can tame the gopher, or ship him to a remote island with no inhabitants. Whatever helps you remember he's not in charge of your thoughts today. You can return to this image whenever anxious thoughts creep up again.

GOD'S GOT THIS

Come to me, all you who are weary and burdened, and I will
give you rest. Take my yoke upon you and learn from me, for
I am gentle and humble in heart, and you will find rest for
your souls. For my yoke is easy and my burden is light.

MATTHEW 11:28–30

Everyone experiences anxious thoughts at one point or another. Anxiety disorders are characterized by persistent fear or worry that is out of proportion to the event at hand. Whether you're dealing with occasional fears or enduring worries, anxiety can make it very difficult to cultivate an optimistic outlook. Anxiety wants to rob us of our joy and tell us our future is uncertain.

So here's a truth for all of us to really lean into and soak down into our hearts: the Lord wants to give us rest. Rest from the fear, rest from the worry, rest from the constant striving and stressing. The God who created the entire universe says, "Come to me." God's got you. He's got every situation you're facing. He knows all about your pain and fear. And he says, "Come. Here is rest for your soul."

REFLECTION Take some time to memorize today's verse. The next time you're feeling anxious or worried, recite it to yourself to remind you that Jesus—gentle and humble in heart, yet powerful beyond measure—is with you, offering rest for your soul. Write out a few things currently stressing you out, then imagine handing those burdens over to Jesus.

HOPE FOR THE FUTURE

Now faith is confidence in what we hope for and assurance about what we do not see. This is what the ancients were commended for.
HEBREWS 11:1–2

A lot of worry is spent stressing out about the future. And while it is important to think about the future—to plan, to act wisely, to consider consequences and outcomes—*considering* the future is quite different than *worrying* over the future.

One of the coolest things about being a follower of Jesus and a believer of the Word is that we already know some really important things that will happen at some point in the future. Christians don't always agree on the specific details, but most have faith Christ is returning to us at some point. We have faith the world will be made new again, and that we will take part in it.

While we don't know how the details of our lives on earth will play out, we know that the end of the big-picture story is pretty awesome— eternity with our Savior. Keeping this in mind during the day-to-day cares of our earthly lives can help put our concerns into perspective.

REFLECTION Have you considered what it will be like to spend eternity in the presence of God? While this doesn't wipe away our concerns for today, thinking about this beautiful future ahead of us can help ease stress. Spend a few minutes pondering an eternity with the Lord.

DAY 37

ALL POSSIBLE OUTCOMES

Do not be anxious about anything, but in every situation, by
prayer and petition, with thanksgiving, present your requests to
God. And the peace of God, which transcends all understanding,
will guard your hearts and your minds in Christ Jesus.

PHILIPPIANS 4:6–7

Whew, this is a tough one: "Do not be anxious about anything." If
anxiety is something you struggle with, this is a very tall order!
But sometimes, a little reframing of your thoughts can help. Sometimes,
just remembering who God is can calm some fears.

God knows absolutely everything—all possible outcomes for any
situation. He knows everything that's ever happened, everything that's
going to happen, everything that *could* have happened but didn't. He
knows literally everything. That thing you're terrified could come to
pass? He's already aware. That thing you *know* is unlikely to happen, but
you keep thinking about it anyway? He's already considered it.

There is nothing that happens outside of God's awareness, nothing
that occurs outside of God's control. You can share your worry with
him, and you can ask for his peace to fill you.

REFLECTION Do you recall a time when something turned out wildly different from the way you expected? Did it occur to you that God knew all along
how that was going to go? Write out some thoughts about that wild detour and
the good things (and perhaps challenging things) that came of it.

PEACE IN THE BODY

Let the peace of Christ rule in your hearts, since as members of one body you were called to peace. And be thankful.

COLOSSIANS 3:15

Like many people, we tend to put a lot of stock in our feelings. If we're not careful, the way we feel about something can begin to define our reality about it. Sometimes this is positive—like when your intuition is correctly telling you to be wary of something, but you don't quite know why yet. But when we're dealing with certain negative emotions—anxiety or shame, for example—our feelings can be liars.

Anxiety, in particular, seems to be on a mission to convince us we're alone. That no one understands us. That everything is scary. That we're never safe. But these feelings are not true. As believers, we can confidently say God is always with us. And more immediately, we can find strength, safety, and peace in a group of trusted believers. We are many members of one body with one purpose—to glorify the God we love!

REFLECTION Take a few moments to prayerfully think about whether fear or anxiety has caused you to push people away. If so, jot a list of ways to connect with some trusted believers, whether that's at your church, online, at school, or elsewhere. If this isn't a problem for you, perhaps ask the Lord to lead you to you someone who's struggling with this. Reach out to that person at your first opportunity.

DAY 39

JUST SAY NO TO BLUDGEONING

When anxiety was great within me, your consolation brought me joy.

PSALM 94:19

Confession: I was really nervous to write anything about anxiety in this book. Culturally, the church hasn't always been great about helping believers who struggle with mental health issues, including anxiety. Verses like many I've quoted have been used as bludgeons to shame those suffering with anxiety and even cast doubt upon their faith and love for Jesus.

If that's happened to you before, I'm so sorry. The verses that encourage us to release anxiety, trust the Lord, shun fear, and find peace should be read as verses of comfort. Verses that remind us we're not alone. That God sees us, and he cares. Verses that support us as we gently retrain our brains and embrace new thought patterns and biblical truths.

Experiencing anxiety does not mean you're broken beyond repair. It means you're a work-in-progress, like every single Christian, being lovingly cared for by our all-knowing, all-seeing, and ever-present Lord.

REFLECTION Have you ever felt shame for experiencing anxiety or another mental health concern? Take a few moments to release that shame during prayer. Everything—*everything*, including our mental health struggles—can be brought before the Lord. We can always approach his throne with confidence!

A VERSE OF EMPOWERMENT

You, dear children, are from God and have overcome them, because
the one who is in you is greater than the one who is in the world.

1 JOHN 4:4

When someone is experiencing an illness, we sometimes say they are fighting it. We fight infection, cancer, and daily chronic health concerns. The same is true with mental illness, including anxiety. And the picture of a battle against an invading army is quite accurate. Some people battle their mental health for a short season. For others, it's a lifelong war.

But remember this, friend: we are not powerless against this foe. Whether it's something we're able to completely conquer, or whether we "win" by learning how to live victoriously and with faith in spite of our ongoing struggles, we are *not* powerless. We have the Holy Spirit within us, helping us in this war. We have our Father, who sees everything, on our side. We have the loving arms of our Savior around us at moments when we feel weak and tired and desperate.

Don't ever stop fighting, friend. You're not alone.

REFLECTION Imagine every tool you have to fight anxiety is embodied in a single weapon. What would your weapon look like? A beautiful broadsword? A nimble bo staff? Write it down or sketch it out. Whenever your anxiety threatens to overwhelm you, picture whatever weapon speaks to you—then go to battle.

OUR GOOD GOD

Taste and see that the LORD is good; blessed
is the one who takes refuge in him.

PSALM 34:8

If you've been a churchgoer for a while—or even your whole life—you have probably heard certain phrases about God over and over. Like "God is good." Or "praise God." But how well do you feel like you *know* God? What do you know about his character? The more we know about who God is at his core, the better we can understand the things we read about him, including his promises, the truths he declares, and the encouragement he's provided in Scripture. Knowing God's character places these often-repeated phrases into deeper context.

What does it mean that God is good? He's kind. Tenderhearted. Gracious toward those who seek him (that's us). And funnily enough, the psalmist who wrote the verse above (our buddy David again) was writing during a time of fear and suffering. Because he knew God so intimately, his response in this time of hurt was to write poetry about the goodness of God. He knew his good, kind God would be alongside him during his season of hardship, and he chose to focus on that truth.

REFLECTION Can you think of a time when God's goodness was apparent to you? Maybe it's in a small moment when you thought back on the day, or there's been a time when a help or solution only God knew about landed in your lap. (I know that is true for me.) When do you feel that our good God sees you and cares?

DAY 42

OUR HOLY GOD

Hang the curtain from the clasps and place the ark of
the covenant law behind the curtain. The curtain will
separate the Holy Place from the Most Holy Place.

EXODUS 26:33

We talked about the Most Holy Place already and how it helps us better understand what it means to approach the Lord's throne. This verse from Exodus is where God gave Moses the instructions for how to build that portion of the tabernacle. It was necessary so the Israelites would understand God's holiness—his complete and utter separateness from sin.

Honestly? It's kind of hard to relate. As fallen humans, we battle our sin. Constantly. The idea of having none of it is pretty foreign to our experience. But not God's. He is the embodiment of holiness. The very opposite of sin. There can be no sin, no wrongness, no mistakes in him because of his holiness.

When we really recognize and understand this part of God's character, it can prompt a variety of responses. But we don't need to be afraid. Remember the promise—we can approach God's throne with confidence (Hebrews 4:16)!

REFLECTION What emotions come to mind when you think of God's holiness? When you think about the fact that God has no wrongness within him, does it help your trust in him begin to grow deeper? Write out your thoughts as you pray through that idea.

OUR MERCIFUL GOD

The LORD passed before him and proclaimed, "The LORD,
the LORD, a God merciful and gracious, slow to anger,
and abounding in steadfast love and faithfulness."

EXODUS 34:6 ESV

Slow to anger." What a wonderful phrase. If we're ever overwhelmed by the idea of God's holiness, we can remember this description of God—slow to anger. Merciful. Patient. Compassionate. These traits sit in perfect balance with his holiness.

He cannot tolerate sin—that's true. His holiness demands he not tolerate sin. But he mercifully sent a savior to us, completing the task we were unable to accomplish. Jesus lived a holy life, yet he took our sins upon himself, allowing us to be reconciled to the Father. And God still helps us day by day, through the hard work of trying to live more and more like our Savior. God's mercy meets us where we are, in our imperfection, brokenness, and immaturity. And not only does he meet us there, he helps us *move on* from our pasts, growing us spiritually and deepening our faith. He is merciful, indeed!

REFLECTION This is going to be tough. Think of the worst thing you've ever done. (Don't worry, you don't have to write it down.) The worst mistake ever—that thing you repented of but still wish you could completely erase. Guess what? God already knows about it. And, mercifully, he has extended forgiveness to you. He loves you just the same. Let that sink in for a moment and write about how that feels.

DAY 44

OUR JUST GOD

He is the Rock, his works are perfect, and all his ways are just.
A faithful God who does no wrong, upright and just is he.

DEUTERONOMY 32:4

The word *justice* can be a little scary. After all, our criminal justice system exists to punish crimes. So when we say God is just, it's easy to immediately jump to "God punishes us." But the words translated as *justice* and *righteousness* in English are part of the same word family in both Hebrew and Greek. When we consider the original languages of the Bible, we can get a fuller picture of what it means to have a "just" God.

God's justice and his righteousness are intertwined. God always does right in every situation. He is the final standard of right and wrong. Unlike our human justice systems, God's justice is perfect. Our weakness might make God's perfect justice seem scary, but we as believers can rest in the knowledge that his justice is always good, fair, and steeped in grace.

REFLECTION God needs to punish sin, but he sent sinless Jesus to take the punishment for *all* sin. Including yours. Have you ever thought about that before—God's justice is satisfied in the sacrifice Jesus made for *you*. Take a few moments to express your gratitude for this amazing gift!

REPLACING BELIEFS: I AM UNWORTHY

For I am convinced that neither death nor life, neither angels nor demons, neither the present nor the future, nor any powers, neither height nor depth, nor anything else in all creation, will be able to separate us from the love of God that is in Christ Jesus our Lord.

ROMANS 8:38–39

As we dive deeper into God's character, we are going to look at some common negative beliefs people carry around. Through our deeper understanding of who God is, we can uproot these negative beliefs (which are lies!) and replace them with truths based on who God says we are.

Sometimes we feel worthless—like nothing we do measures up or no matter how hard we try, we'll never be good enough. And while it's true the Bible says we will never do enough good deeds to earn our salvation (Ephesians 2:8–9) or be as holy as God (Romans 3:23), the truth is that God, in all his goodness, mercy, and grace, says we matter to him (Isaiah 44:2; Proverbs 16:4, Ephesian 1:4). He loves us deeply, wildly, and completely. We didn't earn his love, but simply because we exist and are created in his image, we *matter* to him (Genesis 1:27).

REFLECTION Have you fallen victim to this negative thought before? Have you ever felt worthless? Replace that lie with the truth! You are an adored child of the Most High. Any time feelings of worthlessness creep into your mind, remind yourself of this. And take a moment to write down how that makes you feel now.

REPLACING BELIEFS: I DON'T BELONG

Consequently, you are no longer foreigners and strangers,
but fellow citizens with God's people and also members of
his household, built on the foundation of the apostles and
prophets, with Christ Jesus himself as the chief cornerstone.

EPHESIANS 2:19–20

Everyone feels lonely sometimes. Unfortunately, that's a normal part of being human. But sometimes we can really grab hold of a related but deeper and darker thought: that we simply don't belong. That there isn't a place for us in our family, among our peers, or—worst of all—in God's family.

This lie is such a sneaky, dangerous one. It tempts us to pull away from others, to retreat further into ourselves, to isolate, to hide. But God built humans for community. For relationship. The honest truth is that God wants *everyone* to be part of his family. It doesn't matter if you're shy, or awkward, or if you feel like no one on earth understands you. God sees you. God calls you his child. God says you belong here, with him, with his people.

REFLECTION If you struggle with feeling like you don't belong—or even if you don't deal with that specifically—jot down a list of people you know who you'd like to connect with a little deeper. Think about small ways you might be able to get to know those people better. Intentionally reach out and see if you can expand your community.

OUR OMNISCIENT GOD

*If our hearts condemn us, we know that God is greater
than our hearts, and he knows everything.*

1 JOHN 3:20

You can probably impress someone if you use the fancy theological term *God's omniscience*, but it's actually a very simple concept, just as John states it here. God knows everything. He knows all the big things—the struggles of every people group, the crises of every nation. And he knows all the small things—the intricacies of every heart that ever lived. He knows *everything*.

God is not surprised by current events. Not by wars, pandemics, or the rise and fall of empires. He is not confounded by the sins of humanity. He saw it coming. He sees what's next. And still, he chooses to walk with us—to allow us to walk with him. He offers his love to us, promising never to leave. Because we are not just loved. We are *known* and loved.

REFLECTION What is the deepest, most secret part of yourself? Maybe it's something you struggle with that you've never told anyone about. Or maybe it's something positive, like a dream or creative desire that seems too tender to share with another person. God knows about it. He knows every corner of your heart. Take a moment and write about how that feels.

OUR OMNIPOTENT GOD

"I am the LORD, the God of all mankind. Is anything too hard for me?"
JEREMIAH 32:27

*O*mnipotent—that's another theological vocab word with a very simple meaning. *Omni* means "all," and *potens* means "powerful," so when we say God is omnipotent, it means he's all-powerful.

This trait is so central to God's character, he is sometimes called the Almighty. This name highlights his power. That's who God is—the Lord who is full of ability and authority. He is able to do his holy will in its entirety. There is nothing too hard for him. This is why we sometimes pray for miracles that may sound outlandish to those who don't believe in God. While we know he may choose not to act in the way we ask, we also believe he is *able* to do anything, if it's his will.

In the Old Testament, God's omnipotence was often pointed out when God was being compared to the worthless gods the Israelites were prone to worship. God's power makes him unique among those gods. God's power shows that he is real. When we are in a season of hardship, a season of suffering, or even when we're just trying to deal with the ups and downs of daily life, remembering we are loved by an all-powerful God can encourage, strengthen, and comfort us.

REFLECTION Have you ever considered the vast power of God? If you could ask him to do one thing right now, what would it be? It's cool to think about God's power, but it must always be balanced with the maturity that understands God sometimes chooses not to act, and he is glorified in those times too.

OUR JEALOUS GOD

Do not worship any other god, for the LORD,
whose name is Jealous, is a jealous God.
EXODUS 34:14

God's name is . . . Jealous? Isn't jealousy a bad thing? If we are warned against being jealous, how can God be jealous and sinless?

This is one of those words that, when applied to God, takes on a slightly different meaning than we're used to. When the Bible says God is jealous, it means he wants us to worship him alone. He is jealous for his name, his people, and his reputation.

God is on guard. He knows how he is spoken about and thought of. He knows how his name is treated publicly, and he knows what is hidden in people's hearts. His jealousy will continue to passionately fight against idolatry and rebellion. When human beings are jealous, it's often rooted in sin. God's jealousy is rooted in his own perfect honor. And just like he protects his name, he protects ours.

REFLECTION What are some differences you see between God's jealousy and human jealousy? Consider God's ownership of all creation when you think through this. How does it feel to know that God is jealous to have your worship of him?

OUR BEAUTIFUL GOD

*Whom have I in heaven but you? And earth
has nothing I desire besides you.*

PSALM 73:25

There are a lot of beautiful things on this planet (we will talk about a few of them in a bit). Nature is stunning in its vastness and equally glorious under a microscope. God made mankind like him, capable of love, kindness, creativity, ingeniousness, and goodness. He gave us relationships with other human beings. There's food to enjoy, air to breathe, life to live.

And still, the psalmist says that he desires nothing on earth more than God. Nothing. That's because as wonderful as God's creation is, it pales in comparison to the beauty of the Creator. God is the ultimate expression of all desirable qualities. All good things are found in God to the highest degree possible.

Each of those wonderful things we find on earth reflects God in one or more ways. These earthly reflections give us glimpses into the full and complete beauty of our God.

REFLECTION Jot down a list of five things in this world that absolutely delight you, such as family, friends, food, furry friends. It could be anything that brings you joy. Now think about how each of those things reflects one or more traits of God.

REPLACING BELIEFS: I AM UNLOVED

But God demonstrates his own love for us in this:
While we were still sinners, Christ died for us.

ROMANS 5:8

It's amazing how pervasive this belief is—that we are unloved and unlovable. That no one sees us, cares about us, or gets us. Many people jump into unhealthy relationships with friends or romantic interests because someone, no matter how abusive or unhealthy, has finally made that person feel worthy of attention.

Friend, if you feel this way, let's get one thing straight: those feelings are lying to you. I can say that definitively—without knowing your situations with friends, family, or church—because there is a truth bigger and deeper than all our worldly circumstances. God loves us. And not in the human way. Not in a way that could be revoked, revised, or rethought. Not in a way that's based on a false perception of who we are. God knows every inch of us. And he *loves* us so very much that Jesus went to the cross for us.

REFLECTION If the idea of being unloved is a struggle for you, take the whole week to actively replace that thought every time it pops up. Consider how, though he was well aware of the depth of human depravity, Christ died for us. If you don't struggle with this idea, take a moment to thank God for his amazing love!

REPLACING BELIEFS: I AM BROKEN

He is before all things, and in him all things hold together.

COLOSSIANS 1:17

D o you ever feel like a piece of fabric that has more shreds in it than parts still stitched together? When we're really stressed, upset, frightened, or maxed out, it's easy to feel that way. Sometimes our own sin grieves us so much, we feel irrevocably broken. Beyond redemption.

While it's true in one sense that sin "breaks" us—in fact, I have used the word "brokenness" to describe the human condition at a few points in this book—there is a difference between recognizing our sinfulness and feeling like a broken piece of pottery. Shattered. Unusable. Only fit to be tossed into the trash.

Friend, if weakness and sinfulness disqualified us from being God's adored children . . . no one would qualify. God understands our weakness. He uses our weaknesses at times to display his own power and grace (2 Corinthians 12:9–10), and he mercifully gives us people in our lives who love us as we are, imperfections and all. God holds all things together, including his children.

REFLECTION When you feel like a broken piece of pottery, is there someone in your life who lifts you up? Reminds you of your worth? While we've focused a lot on the biblical truth that God holds us together, it's also important to recognize those in our lives who help remind us of how God sees us.

DAY 53

OUR TRUTHFUL GOD

But the LORD is the true God; he is the living God, the eternal King.
JEREMIAH 10:10

In ancient times, the concept of "true" God would have been understood fairly easily. A multitude of other gods were worshiped in pagan religions, so Jeremiah is highlighting the fact that the God of Israel is the *one* God who is true, living, and eternal. In our culture, idols tend to be things like money, power, success, and anything else we put before our love of God.

God being true also means he is truthful. His words and promises to you never change or fade away. He'll never go back on something he said or flip-flop or mislead you. No human being can meet that standard—not even the most honest person we know! But God is all truth, all the time.

This aspect of God's character is greatly affirming for us. It means he is real, reliable, faithful, and he lives up to his promises. He doesn't lie or change his mind. He *is* truth itself.

REFLECTION Do you struggle with telling the truth? Perhaps write down a few instances where it's tempting to bend the facts, such as when you're confronted with wrongdoing and trying to escape the consequences, or when you feel like you need to boost your reputation. Build up your awareness of these tempting circumstances so you can make truthful decisions when it's hardest for you.

OUR FREE GOD

Our God is in heaven; he does whatever pleases him.

PSALM 115:3

God is perfectly free. He does whatever delights him, whatever is his will, without anyone or anything hindering him. God's power and his freedom work together to bring about his will so that he keeps his truthful promises. See how all aspects of God's character work together?

God's freedom assures us that he will never be thwarted. He is not dependent on others to accomplish what he sets out to do. He is completely free and able to do as he pleases. God has plans for the world—plans for you—and he will make those plans happen.

When we desperately wish something would happen for us and we pray fervently for it, but it doesn't come to pass, we don't need to worry that perhaps something stopped God from carrying out what he *wished* he could do. Instead, we can be assured God has something better in mind for us—and it will happen exactly when it's supposed to!

REFLECTION Sometimes we see God's plans clearest in retrospect. Can you think back to something you thought you wanted but didn't get? Do you now have enough perspective to see what God was doing instead? We don't always get answers about things like this, but sometimes we can see hints, and it's cool to see God's big-picture plan in hindsight!

DAY 55

OUR ETERNAL GOD

"I am the Alpha and the Omega," says the Lord God, "who
is, and who was, and who is to come, the Almighty."
REVELATION 1:8

Our modern world runs on a clock. We have days, weeks, months,
and years to help us keep track of time. These handy segments
allow us to manage our schedules, plan our goals, and even map out
our dreams. Our life is built upon time.

So it's quite outside our personal experience to think about God's
eternity. God has no beginning or end. He's not the first in a series of
created beings. He has *always* existed. Not only did he create everything
that exists, he created time itself. God has always been, and he exists
outside of time. Wow.

Even so, God reaches down to our level to respond to us in time,
as our lives unfold minute by minute. It's one more way God shows us
how much he loves us. He comes down to our level and meets us here,
in our time and space.

REFLECTION We have not always existed in the way God does, but one
of the coolest things about being a follower of Jesus is our souls get to spend
eternity with the Lord. Eternity is a long time—so long, the very thought actually scares some people—but take a few moments to consider what an eternity
of *peace* may be like.

DAY 56

OUR INDEPENDENT GOD

The God who made the world and everything in it is the Lord of
heaven and earth and does not live in temples built by human hands.
And he is not served by human hands, as if he needed anything.
Rather, he himself gives everyone life and breath and everything else.

ACTS 17:24–25

Independence is a highly valued trait in a lot of Western cultures. In the United States, we celebrate the day the colonists declared independence from Great Britain. The idea of freedom to do, say, think, and live as we please is very appealing to us. Maybe that's due in part to humanity's reflection of our Creator's independent nature.

God's independence means he doesn't need anything or anyone. He is completely free of need. Now, don't get offended just yet. God's independence doesn't sound nice, but it's actually pretty cool. He may not need us, but he still *wants* us. He chooses us. He doesn't have ulterior motives or some angle he's playing at. He simply desires relationship with his children. God's independent nature actually shows us how much he cares about us.

REFLECTION Brainstorm a list of some of the gifts and talents God has given to you. Consider how you might use these things to serve, honor, or glorify him in your life.

DAY 57

*The Spirit you received does not make you slaves, so that you
live in fear again; rather, the Spirit you received brought about
your adoption to sonship. And by him we cry, "Abba, Father."*
ROMANS 8:15

It's easy to feel powerless sometimes, especially when you're young. You don't always have control over the details of your life—or the big events. But even when we get older, there's a lot of things outside our control: world events, the behavior of others . . . the weather. The list of things we can't control is nearly endless.

But it's important not to allow feelings of helplessness to overwhelm us. As Christians, we are children of God, and that means we have the strength and agency given to us by the Holy Spirit. We are enabled to do the things God asks. We have the freedom to live boldly. We have the support of God himself behind us as we endeavor to walk like Jesus.

Being empowered to do the Lord's will is no small thing. We may never be able to dictate when it rains or prevent wars from occurring, but we *do* get to make real choices in this life, and those choices can have a ripple effect into others' lives—and into eternity.

REFLECTION Have you ever felt powerless? When those feelings pop up again, replace them with the truth that you are always in control of your own actions. You control how you respond to the things that happen around you. How can you respond in a way that reflects Jesus?

BE FREE

"Then you will know the truth, and the truth will set you free."
JOHN 8:32

The thoughts we allow to play on repeat inside our heads are very powerful. Negative thought patterns—often straight-up lies from the enemy—are like heavy weights on our shoulders. A constant source of sadness, fear, and stress.

Friend, we are not meant to live like that. We are children of God, and we know the *truth*. The truth about who God is. The truth about what he promises us. The truth about how much he loves us. Walking with Jesus doesn't magically make our lives easy. But walking with Jesus does bring the truth into our hearts and minds.

God's truth sets us free. We are free to expel those harmful lies from our thinking. We are free to uproot negative thoughts we've internalized so deeply, we don't even think to question them. You are adored by the Most High. Be free!

REFLECTION Journal daily about your feelings for a while, then review your notes. Do you notice any patterns in your thoughts? Experiencing negative emotions is normal. But if you notice repeating negative thought patterns based on lies (I'm never good enough, I am worthless, etc.), blast those with the truth right now!

OUR OMNIPRESENT GOD

Where can I go from your Spirit? Where can I flee from your presence? If I go up to the heavens, you are there; if I make my bed in the depths, you are there.

PSALM 139:7–8

This verse can bring to mind a funny picture. As though David (the psalm writer) is trying to run away from God, while God's presence is chasing him, continually surprising him at every turn. While we may chuckle at David, sometimes we try the same thing. Hiding from God is certainly not limited to people in the Bible.

But, as David highlights here, God is literally everywhere. It's impossible to flee from his presence. God's omnipresence is a little difficult for us to grasp. It's easy to think of God as filling up the biggest space possible, but that's not quite correct. God created space. There's no space large enough to contain him, and yet he exists everywhere in his creation. It's enough to twist your brain into a knot if you think about it too long.

While it may seem so scary sometimes we want to hide, when we remember God is good, just, loving, and holy, we are reminded that his constant presence is an excellent blessing.

REFLECTION When you think about not being able to hide from God, what emotions rise to the surface? If fear is one of them, consider why that might be. Is there sin you're worried about? Bring it to God now. He already knows, and he's already poised to forgive.

OUR GENEROUS GOD

Every good and perfect gift is from above, coming down from the Father of the heavenly lights, who does not change like shifting shadows.

JAMES 1:17

Followers of Jesus are commanded to be wildly generous with their time, their resources, and their very hearts. We're called to give, to be the hands and feet of Jesus while we wait for him to return. But, as generous as we're meant to be, it's a mere reflection of the generosity that's been bestowed upon us.

All God's traits are like that. You can see his thumbprint on us—his creation—though we don't measure up to his perfection. His generosity is no exception. God is even generous with those who don't know him. The earth's beauty is available for all, not just those who acknowledge the One who made it. As Jesus put it, "[God] causes his sun to rise on the evil and the good, and sends rain on the righteous and the unrighteous" (Matthew 5:45). God gives to humanity as part of his very nature.

Not only can we appreciate the overwhelming generosity God bestows on us, reflecting his generosity to the world around us can boost our spirits, as it shapes us more and more into his image.

REFLECTION How can we reflect God's generosity a little better and a little closer to the way our Father gives? Consider Jesus's words from the Sermon on the Mount (Matthew 5–7) to help you answer this question.

_____

_____

_____

_____

_____

_____

DAY 61

OUR UNCHANGEABLE GOD

They will perish, but you remain; they will all wear out like a garment. Like clothing you will change them and they will be discarded. But you remain the same, and your years will never end.

PSALM 102:26–27

God is the same yesterday, today, and forever. We know this to be true, but maybe we haven't given it much thought. After all, does this truth really affect our daily lives that much?

Absolutely, it does. Can you imagine if God were changeable? What if his standards, his character, his very self, evolved like our world does? What if he was prone to fluctuating emotions and priorities, like the Greek gods? Worst of all, what if the greatest gift you'd ever been given was suddenly taken away because God simply changed his mind?

But none of that will ever happen. God is the same, always. What he promised yesterday still stands. What he said he'd do in the future will surely come to pass. God says he loves you, and he isn't changing his mind.

REFLECTION What are you especially thankful for when it comes to God's unchangeable nature? Take a few moments to reflect upon the permanence of his love, mercy, and goodness.

OUR BLESSED GOD

God, the blessed and only Ruler, the King of kings and Lord of lords, who alone is immortal and who lives in unapproachable light, whom no one has seen or can see. To him be honor and might forever. Amen.
1 TIMOTHY 6:15–16

We hear the word *blessed* a lot in church culture. We usually think about blessings in terms of God's gifts to us. But what does it mean when we say God is blessed?

The Greek word used in this letter to Timothy that is translated as "blessed" (*makarios*) means happiness. Joy. Delight. God's delight is something even deeper and fuller than the delight we experience. His happiness comes from delighting fully and completely in himself. God also delights fully in anything—be it a trait, person, thought, object, or deed—that reflects his character.

Guess what, friend? That includes you. God is happy, joyful, *blessed* when you reflect him. When you walk like Jesus, you delight God. When you're loving and generous, when you make godly choices, when you seek justice and uphold righteousness, God is blessed.

REFLECTION You are a unique person. Each of us is. Have you ever considered the fact that God made you *you* on purpose? Jot down some of your personality traits. What are some ways these traits might bring joy to the Lord?

ROLE MODELS: THE PERSISTENT WIDOW

And there was a widow in that town who kept coming to him
with the plea, "Grant me justice against my adversary."
LUKE 18:3

The persistent widow is a character from one of Jesus's parables. He was using her as an example of how we are to be persistent when we pray to God. In Jesus's story, the widow seeks justice from a corrupt judge who finally grants her request simply because she bugs him so much. Jesus (rightly!) points out that we are not petitioning a corrupt judge but a just, holy, powerful, loving God.

There are other lessons to be found in this story too. Jesus chose a member of society who, at the time, would have been quite powerless. She was a woman, she was without a husband, and chances are she was poor. All of these things would have had a "muting" effect on her voice in society.

But this didn't stop her. She continuously asked the corrupt judge to grant her justice. Like the widow, we can boldly use our voices to seek justice, even when we feel small. We can come to God persistently and know that he will hear us.

REFLECTION Do you have a hard time standing up for yourself or others? Take a few moments to consider why this may be. (For example, sometimes it's wise to be cautious, and other times we let fear stop us from taking important actions.) Now think of one big thing you've been too afraid to ask God for. What might happen if you persistently pursued it?

ROLE MODELS: GIDEON

Then Gideon said to God, "Do not be angry with me. Let me make just one more request. Allow me one more test with the fleece, but this time make the fleece dry and let the ground be covered with dew." That night God did so. Only the fleece was dry; all the ground was covered with dew.

JUDGES 6:39–40

Gideon was an interesting guy who did many great deeds. He led the Israelite army to victory over their oppressors. He also led the people well as a judge in a time before they had a king, and because of all he did to serve God, he is listed as a hero of faith in Hebrews.

But as he was being called into service—knowing he was speaking directly with the Lord—he set up a test so he could be *sure* what God was asking him to do was legit, asking God to show his will by wetting and then not wetting a fleece with dew. (If you ever hear the phrase "putting out the fleece," this is what it refers to.) Gideon was afraid. He wanted to be sure. This mighty man of God was actually timid.

And yet the Lord called him when Gideon felt least assured, most afraid, and most incapable. His uncertainty didn't stop God from using him in powerful ways—because God had certainty in Gideon's strengths, even before Gideon realized what they were.

REFLECTION Do you ever wait to act until you feel absolutely sure you can't fail? What's that one thing you're too afraid to admit you want to attempt? Or the thing you *know* God is calling you to do, but you haven't had the courage to leap into yet? Maybe it's time to take a leap of faith!

DAY 65

THE BEAUTY OF NATURE

*The heavens declare the glory of God; the skies proclaim
the work of his hands. Day after day they pour forth
speech; night after night they reveal knowledge.*

PSALM 19:1–2

When the world feels chaotic, when our personal lives feel unsteady around us, it can be really hard to focus on the positive. Doing so sounds like a good idea, but . . . how? And what does it mean, really, to focus on the positive?

One way to turn our attention to the positive is to look for the beauty around us. God's creation is full of this beauty, and it's free, available to us all the time. The specific wonders around each of us will vary from place to place, but everywhere on earth has its own unique natural beauty. You might have to go to a park or get outside the city to find it, but God's handiwork is never far.

From the splendor of a snowcapped mountain range down to the delicate veins of a tiny leaf, the glory of God's imagination is always on display.

REFLECTION Make an effort to find a little piece of God's natural beauty today. Even if you're not surrounded by nature, this task shouldn't be too hard! It could even be an adorable family pet. God's creation is everywhere!

THE BEAUTY OF HUMANITY

"But a Samaritan, as he traveled, came where the [injured] man was; and when he saw him, he took pity on him. He went to him and bandaged his wounds, pouring on oil and wine. Then he put the man on his own donkey, brought him to an inn and took care of him."

LUKE 10:33–34

People are not always nice. That's no secret. But if we look, we can find many stories of empathy: people helping out in times of need, secretly doing good deeds, or performing random acts of kindness. All these show the beautiful reflection of God in humanity.

The good Samaritan is one of Jesus's parables. He was teaching what "neighbor" really meant. Many Jews then took pride in their heritage, to the exclusion of others around them. Samaritans are thought to be descended from Israelites who intermarried with their Assyrian captors hundreds of years before Jesus told this story. As a result, great tension existed between the Jews and the Samaritans, and both wanted little to do with each other. By using a Samaritan in his story, Jesus was pointing out to his Jewish listeners that the "outsider" who cared for the injured Jew was more of a neighbor than the two Jewish men who passed by the man on the side of the road.

Witnessing acts of kindness—the acts of true neighbors—helps bolster our hope. But we can take it a step further and *be* the reason for hope by reflecting God in how we treat our fellow humans.

REFLECTION Has someone ever done something wildly kind for you? How can you be that wildly kind person for someone else?

THE BEAUTY OF SCRIPTURE

*Above all, love each other deeply, because love
covers over a multitude of sins.*

1 PETER 4:8

I sn't this a lovely verse? Peter encourages us to "love each other deeply." Then he paints a vivid picture—the idea of love covering over our sins. Our mistakes and imperfections are being wrapped up in the grace of those who love us. It's a beautiful thought.

Scripture is full of such language. While we probably miss out on some of the Bible's beauty reading it in English versus the original languages, the Lord graciously preserves many of the allusions, vivid descriptors, deep thoughts, and clever turns of phrase, no matter how it's translated.

If you want to focus on some of the most beautiful words in Scripture, the psalms are a great place to start. They would have been sung originally, so it often feels like reading song lyrics. Another beautiful book is John, as Jesus's close friend gives us a slightly different, more poetic look at the life of our Savior.

REFLECTION Do you have a favorite verse in the Bible? Sometimes our favorites change over the course of our lives, as we focus on different challenges or joys during unique seasons. What verse speaks to your current season? If you're not sure, do some verse hunting by subject to see what resonates.

THE BEAUTY OF ART

He has filled them with skill to do all kinds of work as engravers,
designers, embroiderers in blue, purple and scarlet yarn and fine
linen, and weavers—all of them skilled workers and designers.

EXODUS 35:35

This verse comes from Moses's instructions to the Israelites to build the tabernacle. It was before they entered the promised land. Before the time of the judges. Before the kings. Well before Jesus lived. Which shows God has been recognizing the work and talent of artists for a very long time, and he gave each of us an appreciation for art and beauty.

If you've studied art history at all, you know art has changed a lot through the millennia. And what one person considers beautiful art may be puzzling (or even a little ugly) by another person's standards. But the fact remains that whatever your taste or style, there's art out there for you to appreciate. Maybe you see the beauty in a brilliantly designed building. Maybe you marvel over the skill of the Renaissance painters. Maybe you're blown away by what modern graphic designers are able to do with a tablet, stylus, and design app.

When it comes to art that glorifies God, there's no wrong answer for what's beautiful. Find what speaks to you and notice how it lifts your spirit!

REFLECTION What's your favorite artistic medium? Is your style more modern or classical? Take a bit of time today to notice the art around you. Architecture, photographs, sculptures, paintings, jewelry—it's all art!

DAY 69

THE BEAUTY OF YOUR CREATIVITY

So God created mankind in his own image, in the image of
God he created them; male and female he created them.

GENESIS 1:27

Our God is creative, that's for sure. He is sometimes called the
Creator, after all. That's because where there was once nothing,
God spoke, and then there was something. He spoke things into exis-
tence. And he kept on creating more and more, until Earth was filled
with wonderful—and sometimes fearsome, sometimes unusual, sometimes beautiful—creatures and plants and people.

This creativity is reflected in each of us. Some of us may create the
kind of art we talked about in the last devotion. For others, it might be
something different. Maybe you make music or are a performer of some
kind. Perhaps you build things, grow things, or bake things. You might
tell stories, do crafts, or work with wood, leather, or fabric. And maybe
you're someone whose creativity is best expressed in problem-solving.

No matter what path (or paths) it takes in your life, that creative
spark is a direct reflection of the Creator God who made you. It's just
one more way you bring delight to him.

REFLECTION What are the ways you're most creative? If you feel this area
is lacking in your life, brainstorm a list of creative pursuits that seem interesting
to you. Now pick one to learn about!

70

THE BEAUTY OF LOVE

Love is patient, love is kind. . . . It always protects, always
trusts, always hopes, always perseveres. Love never fails.

1 CORINTHIANS 13:4, 7–8

Just about everyone has love of some kind in their lives—whether it's the love between a parent and child, the love between spouses, the love between friends, or even the love of a pet. Which means it must be a really important part of the human experience.

Scripture talks a great deal about love. God's love, absolutely, but also the love we share with each other. Scripture tells us what love is supposed to look like—patient, kind, protective, hopeful. It tells us what ultimate love looks like in action—laying down our lives for our friends (John 15:13).

Love matters. Jesus said the world would know we're his disciples by our love (John 13:35). It is the hallmark of how we live out our faith in the world and how we treat others. So spread the love!

REFLECTION What are the most loving relationships you have in your life right now? Do they reflect the type of love spoken about in 1 Corinthians? What are some ways you can intentionally nurture the loving relationships you have with family members and friends?

THE BEAUTY OF FRIENDSHIPS

Two are better than one, because they have a good return for their
labor: If either of them falls down, one can help the other up.

ECCLESIASTES 4:9–10

Friendships are vitally important. Example after example in the Bible
shows us this. The bond between David and Jonathan was so strong
that it saved David's life from Jonathan's father, Saul. Hur and Aaron
held up Moses's arms when he grew tired and wasn't able to hold himself up (incidentally, Aaron was also Moses's brother—how wonderful
when our siblings are also our friends!). Paul and Timothy, as mentor
and mentee, worked together for the kingdom.

Friends matter. This wise verse from Ecclesiastes points out that
friends are there to help us when we fall down. When times are hard,
friends are there to lean on. And, in turn, we are there to support them
through their hard times. Friends can be lifelines when we're feeling
overwhelmed.

But friends are also there to share our joys! We celebrate wins and
milestones together. We enjoy laughter, life, and love together. And
sometimes, having friends can make those joys even more frequent.

REFLECTION Do you have close friends in your life who you consistently
lean on? In what ways are you sure to be there for them too? If you don't think
you have friends like this, consider some of the people you get along with well
or would like to know better. What can you do to foster a closer relationship
with those people?

THE BEAUTY OF NEW LIFE

See, I am doing a new thing! Now it springs up; do you not perceive it?
I am making a way in the wilderness and streams in the wasteland.

ISAIAH 43:19

After a long, cold, white winter, the world begins to thaw. The skies warm. The ground melts. Seeds sprout. Green shoots peek up from the soil, ready to fulfill their purpose. Buds open. Flowers bloom. Spring arrives.

Spring is a perfect metaphor for all kinds of new life. Think back to when you first began to follow Jesus—maybe you recall a feeling like spring in your soul during that time. If you've ever seen a newborn baby—or a puppy or kitten, for that matter—you've seen the early stages of new life, and you know the specific beauty of it.

Open possibilities. New beginnings. A clean slate. The exhalation of a long first breath. The beginning of physical life is a one-time event, but we can experience a feeling of spiritual renewal whenever we ask God for rejuvenation in our hearts and minds.

REFLECTION Are you in need of some renewal right now? There's no limit to the number of times you can ask God to give you a fresh start moving forward. If you aren't in that place right now, take time this week to notice the beautiful new life around you or write about something that feels fresh and exciting in your life.

THE BEAUTY OF DIVERSITY

*Just as a body, though one, has many parts, but all its many
parts form one body, so it is with Christ. For we were all baptized
by one Spirit so as to form one body—whether Jews or Gentiles,
slave or free—and we were all given the one Spirit to drink.
Even so the body is not made up of one part but of many.*

1 CORINTHIANS 12:12–14

When God creates, he creates with great variety and imagination. So it's disappointing, to say the least, when people are threatened by diversity. We get very comfortable with people who look like us and think like us. Having shared beliefs, shared experiences, and shared culture is great. But not when it leads us to exclude others who were created in the image of God just as much as we are.

Paul's words are an excellent reminder that God designed the body of Christ to be diverse. From the very beginning, diversity was the intent. Race wasn't a disqualifier. Socioeconomic status wasn't a disqualifier. Having a different gift was not a disqualifier. There is room for everyone at the table, full stop.

And variety is a beautiful thing. Everyone brings a unique point of view, and with it, something new for the rest of us to learn.

REFLECTION Besides humanity, where are places the beauty of diversity stands out to you? A field of wildflowers? The fusion of many cuisines into one great dish? An ecosystem that works together to support itself through the contributions of its many creatures? Look around and write what comes to mind.

THE BEAUTY OF ETERNITY

*He has made everything beautiful in its time. He has
also set eternity in the human heart; yet no one can
fathom what God has done from beginning to end.*

ECCLESIASTES 3:11

God has set eternity in our hearts. Human beings have a sense of something beyond this life, beyond what we can physically experience on Earth, and we have hope that one day we will experience it. And yet, no one can fully understand eternity—not yet, and certainly not as God can understand it.

There's beauty in the mystery of eternity, and there's beauty in the promise that one day, the longing in our hearts will be fulfilled. We will experience what's beyond this life, and we will experience it with our heavenly Father.

When we turn our attention toward the reality of an eternity with God, it helps us remember the temporary nature of our problems in this life. It doesn't mean they're not real or serious—but knowing they aren't permanent does help us gain perspective. The cares of this world are transient. They will pass away, but our souls will endure.

REFLECTION Have you ever thought in depth about eternity? What will it be like, how will it work, what will be the best part? We don't know the details for sure, but contemplating these questions reminds us to keep eternity at the forefront of our minds. It's one of the most amazing, beautiful promises handed to followers of Jesus. Write down a few of your thoughts as a future reminder of the wonderful things God has in store.

DAY 75

EMBRACING EMOTIONS

*A time to weep, and a time to laugh; A time to mourn, and
a time to dance; A time to gain, and a time to lose.*
ECCLESIASTES 3:4-6 NKJV

Exactly halfway through this book seems a good time to address the
idea of "toxic positivity." What is it, and how do we avoid it? Toxic
positivity arises when, no matter how dire a situation is, the person
suffering is encouraged to simply put on a happy face. Keep smiling, no
matter what. Pretend the terrible thing isn't terrible.

If you've ever tried that, you know it's not particularly effective or
healthy. In fact, it can be quite harmful. That type of "positivity" is poi-
sonous. But it's important to distinguish that positivity itself isn't toxic.
It *becomes* toxic when we insist (or others insist) we bury and ignore
our emotions.

The Bible certainly doesn't support the idea that we must deny our
emotions. As the writer of Ecclesiastes says, there is a time to weep.
A time to mourn. Instead of embracing a "grin and bear it" mindset,
we're going to take a look at how to process our emotions in a healthy,
biblically supported way.

REFLECTION Have you ever had the urge to stuff down and deny your
emotions? Perhaps this is the way you've been taught to deal with hard situations. Now is a good time to pray for a mind open to learning a better way—one
that will support emotional and spiritual health, better relationships, *and* a positive mindset.

DEALING WITH OUR COMPLAINTS

*Get rid of all bitterness, rage and anger, brawling
and slander, along with every form of malice.*
EPHESIANS 4:31

Getting rid of conflict and negative emotions sounds amazing ... but how? Stuffing it down and ignoring it isn't the answer, so what is? How do we work through conflict without lapsing into toxic positivity or falling into the bitterness and rage Paul warns against here?

To work through our complaints effectively, we must ask ourselves some questions. First, what am I really upset about? Focus on the facts, and, importantly, identify where you may have erred. This helps you take responsibility for any role you may have played, which then helps resolve conflict. Next ask, what is my desired outcome? Do you want to repair a relationship? Express yourself and be heard?

Last, identify the appropriate person to talk to. Most often, that will be the person you have the conflict with (Matthew 18:15–17). But sometimes, that's not the best option (for example, in cases of abuse). Once you identify who you need to speak to, do so openly, as calmly as possible, and with ears tuned to their point of view.

REFLECTION Are you struggling with a conflict in your life right now? If you have an issue that needs to be addressed, these steps will give you a very clear idea of what you're hoping to accomplish and would like to express. Jot down some notes about it now, then follow through with that loving, healthy discussion.

ALLOWING GRIEF

Record my misery; list my tears on your
scroll—are they not in your record?

PSALM 56:8

It might seem counterintuitive to have a devotion about grief in a book that's supposed to be about positivity. But if we are going to avoid the trap of toxic positivity, it's vital we acknowledge this truth: times of grief, pain, and sadness will come. They do for every single person.

Being a positive person does not mean you have to ignore this fact. That's because being a positive person means that, in spite of our grief and pain, we maintain hope. We maintain joy. We *process* our pain. We don't pretend it isn't there, and we don't allow ourselves to be swallowed by it.

The Bible makes it clear that God knows our grief. He's aware of our pain. He doesn't demand we turn away from those things and act like they don't exist. He does tell us to trust him. To believe in our heart of hearts that he sees us, knows us, and loves us. (Check out Isaiah 41:10 and Jeremiah 29:11 if you need a reminder.) We can—and should—do that while grieving.

REFLECTION Do you have any grief you've been trying to ignore? Friend, that is a heavy burden God doesn't ask you to bear. It's okay to feel it, to process it, and to heal from it. Use the space here to write down how it feels to know God will come alongside you to carry the weight.

ROLE MODELS: JOB

At this, Job got up and tore his robe and shaved his head. Then he
fell to the ground in worship and said: "Naked I came from my
mother's womb, and naked I will depart. The LORD gave and the
LORD has taken away; may the name of the LORD be praised."

JOB 1:20-21

It's impossible to talk about faith during hard times without mentioning Job. He was a person who had everything, including a close relationship with the Lord. But his entire life was turned upside down. His children were killed. His life was destroyed. His good health disappeared.

Job mourned. Job tore his robe in grief. Job sat in misery and repeatedly asked the Lord *why*. His friends rejected him. His wife told him to curse the Lord and die. But Job refused to give up on life—or give up on his faith. And through it all, he also didn't run from the horror of what was happening to him. He looked it in the face and asked, "Why, Lord?" God never answered this question for Job, but he did restore him.

Job's story is a hard one to read, but one of the most interesting lines is Job 1:22: "In all this, Job did not sin by charging God with wrongdoing." Job's story shows us it's okay to grieve. God isn't afraid of our emotions or our questions. But Job was careful about *how* he questioned. He mourned without sinning.

REFLECTION Sadness is not a sin. It's okay to feel things, and it's okay to ask God why and request some insight. Just like it's okay to ask God to give you the strength to carry on. Do you need to ask him about anything today? He's always listening.

SURVIVING HARD TIMES

"Blessed are those who mourn, for they will be comforted.
Blessed are the meek, for they will inherit the earth."

MATTHEW 5:4-5

When things are hard, there's an important question we need to ask ourselves: What, if anything, can I control in this situation? Sometimes we can only control our behavior. Other times, we are able to effect change in hard situations, and in those cases, we have to decide what action we can take and whether or not we wish to do so.

Often, hard seasons prompt us to change one of the most difficult things of all—ourselves. Perhaps a season of loss gives us a new awareness of how short life really is. So we decide to go for all those dreams and plans we've been kicking around for a long time. Or maybe a season of conflict after conflict causes us to work on our mental health in a new way, or work toward a better understanding of ourselves and others in hopes we'll have new peace in our relationships moving forward.

Hard times are not fun. But they can lead to big, positive changes down the road.

REFLECTION What are some big, bold changes you'd like to make in your life right now? Whether or not they were prompted by hard times, we can always choose to better ourselves. Think about some positive goals you'd like to achieve moving forward, then sketch out a plan for how you could get there.

WHEN WE MESS UP

If we confess our sins, he is faithful and just and will forgive
us our sins and purify us from all unrighteousness.

1 JOHN 1:9

No matter how hard we try, no matter how much we focus on healthy communication, good boundaries, or techniques we've learned to support our mental health and that of others, we *will* mess up sometimes. Everyone does. We're not perfect, and that's why we need a Savior in the first place (thank you, Jesus!).

Part of avoiding toxic positivity is being willing to own the negativity we've caused and the harm we've done. In a similar way, part of being mature in our emotional and spiritual lives is admitting our sin—confessing it to God and those we've sinned against, then repenting of it and accepting any consequences.

Whew. Those are *hard* things to do. But it's very necessary we recognize our weakness, acknowledging we don't get it right all the time. The willingness to truly own our mistakes (and repent of them!) will keep our relationships healthy and our consciences clear before God.

REFLECTION Do you have unconfessed sin in your life right now? Something you've been avoiding or ignoring? Let's choose this moment to get clear of it. There is no wrong time to repent. Write down how it feels to let go of that weight.

ROLE MODELS: MARY MAGDALENE

Early on the first day of the week, while it was still dark, Mary Magdalene went to the tomb and saw that the stone had been removed from the entrance.

JOHN 20:1

Mary Magdalene is an epic role model for all Christians. She followed Jesus around Galilee, helped support him financially, served him, and worshiped him. She was at the foot of the cross when Jesus was crucified. She witnessed his burial. She was the first to witness Jesus's resurrection. Jesus chose her to tell the other disciples about his return. You could argue that Mary Magdalene is one of the most devoted followers of Jesus we have record of in Scripture.

But her journey didn't start out that way. She began to follow Jesus after he cast seven demons from her. We don't know much about her life prior to that, but it's easy to imagine living with seven demons was extremely unpleasant. We can also imagine her life of faithful service to Jesus looked very, very different from how she had been living before. Mary's faith journey shows us that sometimes the most powerful testimonies start off in dark places.

REFLECTION Have you ever felt disqualified from a true, deep connection with Jesus? Maybe something about your past has made you feel like you could never be counted among Jesus's most devoted followers. If so, blast that lie right now! No repentant follower of Christ is disqualified. Ever.

Write down some positive thoughts about how being a follower of Jesus now makes you feel, and reflect on what he's done in your life.

BE YOUR OWN FRIEND

Therefore, as God's chosen people, holy and dearly
loved, clothe yourselves with compassion, kindness,
humility, gentleness and patience.

COLOSSIANS 3:12

A lot of people struggle with a constant sense of guilt or shame. Sometimes we feel grief about our own sin, and that can be a positive thing. That grief can lead us to a place of lasting repentance. But shame that constantly accuses, constantly seeks to make us feel unloved and unlovable is not from the Lord. And it can certainly affect our outlook on life, to say the least.

If you ever feel this way, try something: ask yourself how you would advise a friend in your situation. Would you tell her that, yes, she is definitely an irredeemable person? Would you tell him he's beyond hope—a total loser? No way! If your friend had messed up, sure, you would gently point that out. But you would approach your friend with love, compassion, kindness, humility, gentleness, and patience. Can you be your own friend the next time shame tries to accuse you?

REFLECTION If you've been struggling with shame lately, try this exercise. What would you say to a friend in your situation? Write it down, as though you're speaking to that friend right now. When you're finished, read back those words as if they are written for you.

ROLE MODELS: JESUS

When Jesus saw her weeping, and the Jews who had come
along with her also weeping, he was deeply moved in
spirit and troubled. "Where have you laid him?" he asked.
"Come and see, Lord," they replied. Jesus wept.

JOHN 11:33–35

Jesus came to his good friends Martha and Mary of Bethany, whose brother, Lazarus, had died. They had sent word that Lazarus was very sick, and Jesus already knew Lazarus had died before he left for Bethany to see them. But when he saw his friends' grief, he was moved. He wept alongside them.

Jesus is our ultimate role model in many ways. Here, he demonstrates his perfect compassion. He knew what he was about to do—raise Lazarus from the dead. He knew his friend would live and Mary and Martha were about to have their brother returned to them. And still, he was touched by their grief. He grieved with them. Unlike Job's friends, who poked at his sensitive spots as he grieved, insisting he must have sinned (he hadn't), Jesus cried with his friends.

While we do not have Jesus's power to perform miracles or his ability to know what's going to happen next, we do have the power to choose compassion.

REFLECTION Is there someone in need of extra compassion this week? A friend or loved one? Perhaps you're in need of extra compassion right now too. Write down their names (or if it's you, your needs) and be intentional about showing the kind of empathy Jesus did.

MERELY HANGING ON

Consider it pure joy, my brothers and sisters, whenever you face trials of many kinds, because you know that the testing of your faith produces perseverance.

JAMES 1:2–3

If you scroll social media for any length of time, it's easy to get the impression that most people out there are living an awesome life. Rocking all their goals. Looking perfect all the time. Consistently saying just the right witty, funny, or poignant thing.

It's easy to forget these impressions are coming from highly curated, intentionally posed, staged, or even manipulated snapshots into small windows of someone's life. It's not the whole story. It's not the whole picture. You don't have to be rocking out at life all the time in order to be happy, joyful, or positive. Sometimes, it's okay to merely hang in there through trials, hardships, persecution, conflict, and even everyday life—which can be hard enough on its own.

Remember—hard times are real, but they are often temporary. Just doing the best you can in those moments might not look or feel glamorous. But it strengthens your faith and your resilience, carrying you through to a happier season.

REFLECTION Have you ever felt like you have to have it all together to be happy? Have you ever thought, "If only [fill in the blank], *then* I will be able to feel peace, happiness, or fulfillment"? Let's release that idea. Right now is the time to start pursuing the peace and fulfillment you desire, with Christ as your steadfast foundation. What does *that* fill-in-the-blank look like?

ROLE MODELS: PAUL AND ONESIMUS

So if you consider me a partner, welcome [Onesimus]
as you would welcome me. If he has done you any
wrong or owes you anything, charge it to me.

PHILEMON 17–18

The book of Philemon is short and not particularly well-known. It's just one chapter—more of a quick note than a book. But in it, we find a fascinating snapshot of the intersection of three lives: Paul, who is writing the letter; Philemon, the recipient of the letter and a fellow believer; and Onesimus, Philemon's slave who had run away.

After running away, Onesimus had come to faith in Christ after spending time with Paul. Paul then sends Onesimus back to Philemon with the note we now know as the book of Philemon, urging Philemon to forgive Onesimus and receive him not as a slave but as a brother. The main takeaways for us here are the brotherhood of all believers and the beauty of reconciliation between two believers.

If you've ever felt like someone who has run away from God and must return to him, repentant and unsure how you will be received, this story should give you hope! Paul's words to Philemon—how he asks Philemon to receive Onesimus as a "beloved brother in the Lord" (v. 16)—reflect God's heart for all of us.

REFLECTION Do you recall a time when you've been (figuratively) in Onesimus's position? Or perhaps you've been in Philemon's shoes, facing a person who wronged you but is now repentant. Write about how this story might shape your responses in the future.

LOVING OUR BODIES

*I praise you because I am fearfully and wonderfully made;
your works are wonderful. I know that full well.*

PSALM 139:14

There's a lot of pressure on both guys and girls when it comes to how we look. In recent years, there have been efforts to encourage body positivity and realistically present photos of models and celebrities, and to educate people about the ill effects of some of our culture's beauty standards (eating disorders and overall self-perception, to name two).

And yet, "face-fixing" filters are readily available on most social media apps and cell phone cameras. Plastic surgery is the norm in Hollywood. For many, superficial beauty is still the standard by which we judge a person's worth.

These harmful messages run counter to what the Bible tells us is true. God made each of us, fearfully and wonderfully. He created us, exactly as we are, on purpose. Our bodies are magnificent creations, capable of amazing things, beautiful in their uniqueness. It honors God when we treat our bodies well—when we love them well and recognize them as the glorious creations they are.

REFLECTION Are you prone to nitpicking things you dislike about your body? Shift your focus to the things you do like about your body. Maybe there are features you particularly like—a great smile, adorable freckles, glowing skin. Maybe there are amazing things your body is able to do (even just breathing is pretty amazing, to be honest). Write them down!

SWEET SLEEP

*When you lie down, you will not be afraid; when
you lie down, your sleep will be sweet.*

PROVERBS 3:24

Taking care of our bodies is directly connected to maintaining a positive, healthy outlook and allowing our brains to function optimally. Science proves it, and we'll dive into that later. We'll also look at ways to take care of our bodies. But everyone agrees—researchers, doctors, your teachers, your parents—that good sleep is essential.

Sleep allows our bodies to rest and repair cells. The brain stores information and gets rid of waste. Muscles relax. Breathing slows, blood pressure drops, and specific hormones are released. We work as designed.

Jesus promised rest to the weary and burdened (see Matthew 11:28), and while he was talking about rest for our souls, the idea of *rest* is reinforced a number of times in the Bible. Even God rested from his work (Genesis 2:2). Here are some ideas for improving sleep:

- Have a consistent bedtime and wake-up time
- Limit screen time in the hours before you sleep
- Use a blue-light filter on your devices in the evenings
- Don't consume caffeine later than the afternoon

REFLECTION Are you struggling with poor sleep? Write out a plan for improving your sleep. You can use the list above as a starting point, or craft your own based on your research and personal habits.

EDIFYING EATING

So whether you eat or drink or whatever you
do, do it all for the glory of God.
1 CORINTHIANS 10:31

It's interesting that under the God's original covenant in the Old Testament, what people ate mattered to God. Certain things were off limits, and other things were deemed "clean." These restrictions have been removed for followers of Christ (Acts 10:9–16), but we can still gather some wisdom from those Old Testament laws: we should pay attention to what we put in our bodies.

It's wonderful to have the freedom to choose what we eat, but with that freedom comes a lot of potential for unhealthy habits. Everyone's body is a bit different. Different percentages of carbohydrates, protein, and fat will be optimal for one person but not another depending on their health situations. Different bodies have vastly different caloric needs. But there are some things we know are not healthy for anyone. Lots of processed sugar and deep-fried foods are great as occasional treats, less great as two of your core food groups.

Remember you get one body in this life, and the better fuel you give your body, the better it can run!

REFLECTION Do you feel like you need to create some balance in your eating habits? Perhaps there's a positive goal you'd like to work toward— eating more vegetables, drinking more water, experimenting with new sources of protein. Write down some of your health-related goals now, then break those goals down into small, actionable steps to help you get started.

HEALTHY HYGIENE

See, I have taught you decrees and laws as the LORD my
God commanded me, so that you may follow them in
the land you are entering to take possession of it.

DEUTERONOMY 4:5

Maybe this is an odd verse to use when talking about hygiene, but the actual verses in the Law about the topic get pretty specific. God had things to say to the Israelites about sores, blood, rashes, dead bodies, and excrement. Not the most inspirational reading, but it's interesting to note how God's laws about personal hygiene and various medical situations helped protect his people from microorganisms, which would not be discovered by human beings until the 1600s.

The point? When we talk about taking care of our physical bodies for the sake of our mental health, hygiene should get some consideration. God thought it was worth mentioning in the Law, after all. The ability to wash in clean water—to have access to soap, toothpaste, and deodorant—is actually a huge blessing that gets overlooked sometimes. If you've always had access to these things, it's easy to think of them as givens, but for many across the world, they're not. Personal hygiene can sometimes feel like a chore, but it's an important part of looking and feeling our best.

REFLECTION Do you think of personal hygiene as more chore than blessing? Take a moment to reframe those thoughts based on the fact many people throughout history didn't have access to the things we have now—and there are still those today who don't. Are there some things that could transform this task from chore to self-care? A fun soap or bubble bath?

FUNCTIONAL FITNESS

She sets about her work vigorously; her
arms are strong for her tasks.

PROVERBS 31:17

A lot of fitness talk is focused on achieving a certain aesthetic—slimming down, bulking up, toning, sculpting . . . There's no shortage of opinions about the best way to work out, the best way to achieve the look you're going for.

But none of that is really the point of fitness. The point is health. Wellness. Strength—whatever that means for your body and your ability. Our bodies are made to move, and in our modern world of constant entertainment (often done in front of a screen), it's easy to neglect this.

Physical activity doesn't have to take place in a gym. In fact, all the better if it doesn't! Enjoying a walk, a hike, playing sports, going for a swim—these are all awesome options for getting your wonderfully created body moving while enjoying God's handiwork outside.

REFLECTION What's one fitness- or activity-related goal you can begin to work on this week? If this isn't a part of your normal life, don't be embarrassed to start with something small. Remember, the point is to keep your cardiovascular system healthy, your muscles strong, and your endorphins up.

PRACTICING FORGIVENESS

*Be kind and compassionate to one another, forgiving
each other, just as in Christ God forgave you.*

EPHESIANS 4:32

One of the very best—but sometimes very hard—things we can do for our mental health is to forgive others. This is *difficult*, friends. At least, it can be. When someone has hurt us, the natural human thing to do is hold on to that hurt. To desire revenge. To refuse to let it go. To let the offense fester.

But not only is this harmful to your heart and harmful to your mental health, it's also the exact opposite of what the Bible instructs us to do. Let's be clear—this does *not* mean you must continue to put yourself in an abusive situation (never!). This does not mean you must continue to be in fellowship with someone who unrepentantly sins against you. But it does mean those who are repentant should be shown grace. It does mean that, even when someone else continues on in their sin, we can choose to release anger, hurt, and bitterness.

Forgiving others is sometimes about them, but it's always about us. However they respond to our forgiveness, being a forgiving person benefits our mental well-being.

REFLECTION Are you holding on to unforgiveness against someone? Take some time to think and pray through it. Has this person repented? Are they a brother or sister in Christ? Dive deep into the heart of the situation, then ask God how he wants you to move forward.

PURPOSEFUL YOU

For we are God's handiwork, created in Christ Jesus to do
good works, which God prepared in advance for us to do.
EPHESIANS 2:10

Have you ever seen someone knit, stitching together a garment from a pattern and a ball of yarn, piece by piece, then sew it all together? Or perhaps you've watched someone embroider something—the many tiny stitches coming together to spell a word or create a beautiful image.

That's one picture that comes to mind when we say the word *handiwork*. And it's an appropriate one, as God has pieced each of us together, stitch by stitch, trait by trait. He *made* us. We're his special creations, his handiwork. Scientifically speaking, yes, we are a result of our genetic makeup. But Scripture tells us God is intimately involved in this process. He knows each of us. He prepares works for us to do ahead of time.

He created you *on* purpose and *for* purpose. You are not a mistake. You are just as you were intended to be.

REFLECTION Without thinking too hard, write down ten things you like about the way the Lord created you. What traits did he give you that you appreciate? What parts of you do you find helpful, useful, beautiful? He delights in you, friend, and it's okay to share that delight with him!

IDENTIFY YOUR STRENGTHS

We have different gifts, according to the grace given to each of us.
ROMANS 12:6

Paul tells us in Romans that we each have different gifts. And from Ephesians 2:10, we know we have good works to do that the Lord prepared for us ahead of time. It's safe to assume those good works will utilize the gifts he's given to us. Sometimes he'll call us outside our comfort zones and ask us to do something we might feel unequipped or unprepared for. But most of the time, the Lord directs us toward work we're built for.

Have you ever thought about what those gifts, those strengths, are for you? We use our spiritual gifts to serve the kingdom of God, of course, but it's also wise to consider how we might use our skills and talents in our education and career pursuits. It's wise to think about how we can lean into our God-given identities to help our friends, strengthen our relationships with family members, and reach out to our communities. When we use our gifts, not only are we improving the world around us and helping others, the process boosts our mood by helping us feel useful, productive, and purposeful.

REFLECTION Remember the list of things you like about yourself you created in the last devotion? I bet you wrote down some of your natural strengths. Revisit that list now to see what you wrote. What themes do you see? How can you use those strengths to glorify God in one or more areas of your life?

IDENTIFY YOUR INTERESTS

Whatever you do, work at it with all your heart, as
working for the Lord, not for human masters, since you
know that you will receive an inheritance from the Lord
as a reward. It is the Lord Christ you are serving.

COLOSSIANS 3:23–24

We are each gifted with a unique personality and special gifts. These lead to—but are distinct from—our interests. Our interests are the things that light us up inside. The stuff we geek out about. The activities we love. The topics we could talk about for hours if we find someone who shares that interest.

Some of these interests will flow in and out of our lives as we get older and move on to other things. Some of them will be lifelong passions. Pay attention to the things that excite you. This is part of your unique identity, and it might be an area God eventually calls you to (like if you were an avid reader all through your childhood, you may be called to write devotionals—just as a random example!).

Discovering who you are is a journey that can take a while. A lifetime, in fact. But God created you intricately and purposely. His handiwork is worth examining.

REFLECTION Quick, name five things you are absolutely passionate about. Maybe there's an obvious kingdom-service connection (like if you said "singing worship music"), or maybe those connections are less obvious (baking stellar cupcakes, playing soccer, reading novels). Whatever you love, think about how you can be a light for the kingdom while engaged in those activities.

ROLE MODELS: MARTHA OF BETHANY

Jesus said to her, "I am the resurrection and the life. The one who believes in me will live, even though they die; and whoever lives by believing in me will never die. Do you believe this?" "Yes, Lord," she replied, "I believe that you are the Messiah, the Son of God, who is to come into the world."

JOHN 11:25–27

Martha gets a bad rap sometimes. She's the "busy sister," the one who was so annoyed that her sister Mary was sitting at the feet of Jesus, listening to him teach instead of helping her host their dinner party. Then she basically demanded Jesus rebuke her sister (yikes—relatable, but yikes). So, yes, she had her issues, but focusing *only* on that event neglects the full story of one of the few New Testament women who gets several mentions.

Martha was a good friend and a devoted follower of Jesus. And she was among the first of Jesus's followers to recognize who he is—the Messiah. Even if she didn't fully understand what that meant until after Jesus died and was resurrected, Martha *believed*. She got it. She got it better than some of Jesus's twelve disciples. Her confession of faith here in John 11 is nearly identical to Peter's in the other three gospels. Martha wasn't perfect. But she understood.

REFLECTION Are you prone to the kind of busyness and frustration Martha showed in her most famous story? Many people are full of constant demands, especially in our hectic world. Remember, those foibles do not mean you can't also have deep faith in the Lord. Martha did. What can you do to take a moment to focus on the bigger things?

ROLE MODELS: PETER

[Peter] denied it again, with an oath: "I don't know the man!"
After a little while, those standing there went up to Peter and said,
"Surely you are one of them; your accent gives you away." Then
he began to call down curses, and he swore to them, "I don't know
the man!" Immediately a rooster crowed. Then Peter remembered
the word Jesus had spoken: "Before the rooster crows, you will
disown me three times." And he went outside and wept bitterly.

MATTHEW 26:72–75

On the surface, this passage doesn't show Peter as a role model. We certainly don't want to emulate him here—denying his close relationship with Jesus because he's afraid. But the fact Peter's story includes his great faith as a disciple, his sometimes rash behavior, his denial, and his ultimate service to God should bring us great hope.

Why? Because Peter is like us. He has a temper. He isn't always brave. He gets frustrated, his feelings get hurt. He insists he won't do something, then does it. Peter is extremely human. And Jesus chose him anyway—not only as a disciple, but as one of his closest friends and the man who would lead the church after Jesus left. Peter gives us hope for what our own lives can be, despite our imperfections.

REFLECTION Is there a very human Bible hero you find relatable? Peter, Moses, Sarah, and David are just a few examples who are painted in flaws-included detail. What do you think it means that God saw fit to include these people, with all their weaknesses and mistakes, in the biblical narrative?

ROLE MODELS: DEBORAH

Now Deborah, a prophet, the wife of Lappidoth, was leading Israel at that time. She held court under the Palm of Deborah between Ramah and Bethel in the hill country of Ephraim, and the Israelites went up to her to have their disputes decided.

JUDGES 4:4-5

Since we're talking about using your talents, gifts, and interests to lean into the unique identity and work God has prepared for you, let's look at Deborah. She was an ancient Israelite. She lived in a male-dominated culture. And she was a prophet and judge. When Israel was being attacked, a man named Barak was commanded to lead Israel's army, and Deborah was so trusted, so wise, so connected to the Lord that Barak refused to go into battle unless she went with him. Wow.

The Bible doesn't shy away from her role. Though her position was unusual, Scripture states it matter-of-factly: she was a prophet leading Israel, and she held court to decide the matters of the people.

God's calling doesn't always fit with our culture or the expectations of others. It's vital to follow the leading of the Lord and the examples set for us in Scripture to help us determine what God asks of us, rather than leaning on what others expect of us.

REFLECTION Have you ever been called to do something outside your comfort zone? Or, more like Deborah, are the things you're called to exactly in the zone of your gifts, but those gifts don't necessarily line up with what others might expect? How have you handled this in the past, and how can you push forward now knowing God gifted you for a purpose?

BE LIKE JESUS

"You call me 'Teacher' and 'Lord,' and rightly so, for that is
what I am. Now that I, your Lord and Teacher, have washed
your feet, you also should wash one another's feet. I have set
you an example that you should do as I have done for you."

JOHN 13:13–15

Jesus is our ultimate example. Perhaps that goes without saying, but in a book that aims to help us cultivate a positive, healthy mindset, we must look at our ultimate teacher for guidance about how to live our lives. Guidance about how to focus on the right things.

Look, we're never going to reach Jesus's level of perfection in anything. If we set that unattainable standard for ourselves, we'll go crazy over the depth of our failure. But our inability to do something perfectly does not excuse us from the effort. Jesus said, "I have set you an example." Actively shaping ourselves to look like Christ not only furthers the kingdom, it also enriches our lives. We will look at several specific ways we can be like Jesus, but remember that as a general rule, when you're reading Scripture, if you see Jesus modeling it, it's a good thing for you to do!

REFLECTION When you think about what you know of Jesus, what is his most amazing trait, in your opinion? There's no wrong answer, just what resonates most for you. (If it helps you get started, I love how Jesus reaches out to those his society overlooked—the poor, the sick, the afflicted.)

PRIORITIZING THE FATHER

After three days they found him in the temple courts, sitting among the teachers, listening to them and asking them questions. Everyone who heard him was amazed at his understanding and his answers. When his parents saw him, they were astonished. His mother said to him, "Son, why have you treated us like this? Your father and I have been anxiously searching for you." "Why were you searching for me?" he asked. "Didn't you know I had to be in my Father's house?"

LUKE 2:46–49

I identify with Mary here. If I suddenly realized my twelve-year-old son was missing, I would be beside myself. The panic!

But setting aside the stressful moment, there's an awesome example here. Even as a boy, Jesus had his priorities straight. He made a point to be in his Father's house. He focused on God's Word—studying it, interpreting it, discussing it. He knew what mattered in life.

Sometimes older generations look down on younger ones. But they shouldn't. Paul writes, "Don't let anyone look down on you because you are young, but set an example for the believers in speech, in conduct, in love, in faith and in purity" (1 Timothy 4:12). Jesus's example and Paul's encouragement to young Timothy show us that young people can be focused believers with excellent priorities—examples for anyone of any age.

REFLECTION What is one thing you can do today to become more serious about studying God's Word? Do you need to spend more time in each book, digging into the content? Or cover more ground in your Bible, reading books you've never read before? Other ideas? Write them down!

LOVE YOUR ENEMIES

"You have heard that it was said, 'Love your neighbor and hate your enemy.' But I tell you, love your enemies and pray for those who persecute you, that you may be children of your Father in heaven."

MATTHEW 5:43–45

Oof. This is tough, there's no way around it. Jesus's command in Matthew 5 pokes at a very tender place in our humanity. When we're wronged, we tend to want vengeance. The Law even laid out exactly how retribution should take place—what was appropriate to seek, what was not. Humans tend to *want* an eye for an eye, a tooth for a tooth.

But you may notice the word I used above—*command*. It's not optional to show love to your enemies if you're a follower of Christ. Even (and especially) those enemies who actively persecute you. Double oof. Again, this does not mean we must keep ourselves in abusive situations or sit silently while we—or others—are being harmed. But it doesn't leave any room for revenge. Or bitterness. Or malice. These things not only damage our witness for Christ, they harm our hearts. A heart filled with rage is not a heart that reflects our example, Jesus.

REFLECTION You know what I'm going to say. Take a few moments to pray for someone who has persecuted you. Unrepentant evildoers will face justice one day, and that justice belongs to the Lord. *Our* job is to pray, to show the love of Christ, and to keep shaping our own lives in the image of his.

LEAD WITH COMPASSION

When he saw the crowds, he had compassion on them, because
they were harassed and helpless, like sheep without a shepherd.

MATTHEW 9:36

You probably show compassion on a regular basis, even if you don't realize it. Whether it's for a hurting friend, an injured animal, or a sick relative, you have likely shown compassion to someone in need recently. It's a normal, healthy response when we see someone who needs help. So what is the difference between our compassion and Jesus's?

Jesus didn't just regularly show compassion. He *continually* showed compassion. He didn't only show mercy to those his culture accepted. In fact, he actively sought the marginalized. He healed the sick and suffering. He touched those his society shunned. He reached out to sinners and showed them God still cared. He actively challenged the religious leaders of the time, and that was an act of compassion for both the leaders—who were given the chance to repent—and those who were living under those leaders' heavy, ungodly burden.

For Jesus, compassion was a continual state of being.

REFLECTION What are some ways you can show compassion to others beyond what you usually do? Think about the marginalized groups in your society who might need love and kindness. Compassion is built on the simple act of *caring* and taking an open, active interest in others.

UNCOMPROMISING TRUTH

"I am the way and the truth and the life. No one
comes to the Father except through me."

JOHN 14:6

Being a compassion-forward person does not mean compromising the truth. Sometimes we struggle to strike a balance between those two things, leaning too heavily on accepting everything in the interest of being kind, or leaning too heavily on screaming the truth as we understand it at all passersby, thinking we're helping them somehow.

If we want to know how to be truly compassionate, we only need to look at Jesus's example. (Sensing a theme?) More often than not, Jesus paired the unflinching truth with a compassionate act. He saved an adulterous woman from being stoned to death—showing compassion, mercy—and then told her to leave her life of sin—presenting truth, holiness.

We won't do this perfectly. We'll mess up on achieving this balance. But the more aware we are of attempting to walk in Jesus's footsteps, the better chance we have of at least hitting the target. Remember, above all, Jesus served his Father by loving people.

REFLECTION What do you think are the three most important truths of Christianity? That's a big question! And answers may vary, but toward the very top of your list should be something that acknowledges Jesus as our Lord and Savior.

PERFECT PATIENCE

Then Peter got down out of the boat, walked on the water
and came toward Jesus. But when he saw the wind, he was
afraid and, beginning to sink, cried out, "Lord, save me!"
Immediately Jesus reached out his hand and caught him.
"You of little faith," he said, "why did you doubt?"

MATTHEW 14:29–31

Sometimes we read stories in the Bible and shake our heads. The Israelites seemed to constantly wander from God, who repeatedly revealed himself to them—and who proved over and over how faithful, powerful, and merciful he was. The disciples, bless them, seemed intent on misunderstanding Jesus at times. For how closely they physically followed him, they didn't *get* Jesus until very late in the game.

We shake our heads, and yet . . . we are exactly the same. We have the Holy Spirit *dwelling inside us*, and still we mess up frequently. We stubbornly follow our own ways, rather than submitting to God's better ways. We are as stubborn as the Israelites, as clueless as the disciples.

But God's still with us. Sticking by us. Correcting us, convicting us, encouraging us. Because the Lord is patient with his children—delaying judgment and training us, growing us, as we work to be more like him.

REFLECTION Do you relate to the disciples and the Israelites? Do you feel you make the same mistakes over and over? Write out some bad habits and patterns you find yourself falling into, and brainstorm ways to improve in those areas. Give yourself grace on that journey—because the Lord does!

SURRENDER TO GOD'S WILL

"Father, if you are willing, take this cup from
me; yet not my will, but yours be done."

LUKE 22:42

This is one of the most fascinating verses in the Bible. These are words Jesus prayed in the garden of Gethsemane the night before his crucifixion. He was about to be arrested. Knew he was going to die. Knew *why* he had to die. And . . . he didn't want to. His human desire was to be spared that pain—physical, emotional, and spiritual.

But he didn't stay stuck in his own human desire. He didn't pray, "Father, please make this your will." He prayed, "Not my will, but yours be done." Whatever you will, Father, is best. *Your* will be done.

Wow. It's a simple statement from Jesus, yet so profound. He was facing a tremendous, awful, important task, and he submitted to the Father's will. We are not asked to do anything as difficult as what Jesus faced. Yet we are asked to do hard things. Painful things. Things that are important but require the kind of strength that can only come from God. May Jesus be our example.

REFLECTION In order to surrender to God's will, the most important thing we have to do is trust him. Is there anything you're feeling fearful or unsure about in your life? Any huge decisions coming up? Pray about them now, asking God to give you a strong sense of the best choice you can make in these situations, as well as the power to obey that direction.

SUBVERTING THE ESTABLISHMENT

When the teachers of the law who were Pharisees saw him eating
with the sinners and tax collectors, they asked his disciples: "Why
does he eat with tax collectors and sinners?" On hearing this,
Jesus said to them, "It is not the healthy who need a doctor, but
the sick. I have not come to call the righteous, but sinners."

MARK 2:16–17

Let's start off with the disclaimer that we're not encouraging anarchy here. What we *are* encouraging is what Jesus did—he challenged the cultural norms of his day. He poked at the religious leaders (and stood up to them when they tried to poke him). He pointed out their hypocrisy and greed. He hung out with people they didn't approve of, and he showed the love of God to those people, often with heart-changing results.

Of all the things Jesus did on earth, this is perhaps the one we must approach with the most discernment, wisdom, and caution. Human hearts like to rebel sometimes, and it's important we don't rebel for rebellion's sake. But when we subvert cultural standards that are ungodly and hypocritical, even if they are wrapped in religious language and tradition, we are following in the footsteps of our Savior.

REFLECTION Does "subverting the establishment" sound like a scary concept? It can be. This is why we must use wisdom when emulating Jesus in this area. What are some ways you can get started? Start a list here. A good place to start could be reaching out to the marginalized in your society, and practicing grace. Be cautious when flipping any tables, though (Matthew 21:12–13).

PRACTICE OF PRAYER

But Jesus often withdrew to lonely places and prayed.
LUKE 5:16

Jesus lived a life of prayer. We can only speculate what it was like in Jesus's head. He was fully human, so his thought processes would be somewhat familiar to us (though they'd probably look different than ours because he had no sin!). But he was deeply connected to the Father because he was also the Son of God. He knew the Father's will. And, through prayer, he talked to his Father all the time.

This verse says Jesus "often" withdrew to lonely places. Places where the demands of the crowds weren't pressing. Places where the disciples weren't asking so many questions. Places where he could have silence. Not that Jesus minded questions or requests for healing and help. But the space to be able to hear himself think and talk to the Father was obviously important to him too.

Likewise, our lives are busy, noisy, and full of demands, but it's really important we find quiet places—both physically and mentally—to connect with God the way Jesus did so we can recharge.

REFLECTION Have you created space for silence, where you can pray without the demands of the world pressing in on you? Identify a specific time this week—daily, if possible!—to set aside time for silence so you can pray. It doesn't have to be a ton of time. Just a little window that's for you and God, alone.

KINGDOM FIRST

"But seek first his kingdom and his righteousness, and
all these things will be given to you as well."
MATTHEW 6:33

You've probably heard this verse before. But what does it mean to seek God's kingdom and his righteousness first?

This verse is in the middle of Jesus's famous Sermon on the Mount. He was drawing distinctions between the kingdom of God and worldly living. Specifically, this verse is contrasting our worldly concerns (which are still important—what we will eat, what we will wear, etc.) with our heavenly ones. This is not to say Jesus doesn't think we should eat or wear clothes (please, do wear clothes). But it does mean those temporary, earthly things shouldn't be our main focus in life. We should not be seeking these things above and before the kingdom of God. This verse is about where Jesus says our focus should be.

Instead of letting yourself get consumed by everyday concerns, search out the kingdom. Become curious about it. Dig into Scripture. Pray often, and think about what you've read and prayed about.

REFLECTION On a scale of one to ten, how kingdom-focused have you been lately? Have the cares of the world been consuming you instead? It's tough to keep redirecting our focus to the kingdom in times of stress or pain, but this practice is an important way to keep our priorities focused in the right place—and on the right Person.

BUILDING THE BENEFICIAL

"I have the right to do anything," you say—but not everything is beneficial. "I have the right to do anything"—but I will not be mastered by anything.

1 CORINTHIANS 6:12

The Christian life, in some ways, gives us a lot of freedom. We live under grace, knowing we don't have to strive to earn our salvation. We don't need to panic when we make mistakes, as we know God is quick to forgive his repentant children. There's soul-deep freedom in that. God's got us, all the time.

But that doesn't mean everything is beneficial for us. As Paul points out here, we may be *able* to do anything in the sense we have confidence in our salvation and ability to be forgiven. But many things that are available to us are not healthy. Not good. Not beneficial.

Over the next few days, we're going to take a look at several things that are good—good habits and practices that turn our attention toward God and help us cultivate a positive outlook in our lives. These habits are built on biblical wisdom, but they are practical, concrete, attainable goals you can put into practice now.

REFLECTION A good first step in building good habits is weeding out any bad habits that might be lurking in our lives. Is there something that springs to your mind when you see the phrase *bad habit*? What can you do today to start uprooting that habit from your life?

DAY 109

PERPETUAL PRAYER

Pray continually.

1 THESSALONIANS 5:17

Didn't we just talk about prayer? Yes! But it's that important. Paul says here to pray *continually.*

Sometimes we think of prayer as asking a question. We need or want something, so we ask God for it. We ask him to intervene in a situation, to grant us wisdom, to give us something. And those prayers are just fine in those moments. But if we want to build a continuous prayer life, it's important to think of prayer as something more than an "asking session."

When we pray continually, we pray our thanks. God has richly blessed each and every one of us, and it has nothing to do with our finances or the things we have. When we move through life always acknowledging the source of goodness, kindness, grace, love, and holiness, we are in a different kind of continuous prayer. When we are always aware of our dependence on God, we are in continual prayer.

REFLECTION These reflections often say, "Take a few moments to pray . . ." Today, we're going in a different direction. Instead of taking a few moments, spend the day in prayer, but not in the "asking session" way. Do the things you usually do throughout the day, but with a constant awareness of God's goodness and your dependence on him. Make some notes on the overall experience. What steps can you take to turn this practice into a regular habit?

LEARN TO LAUGH

**A cheerful heart is good medicine, but a
crushed spirit dries up the bones.**
PROVERBS 17:22

Humor has been shown to have a positive impact on our outlook. There's even a term for joking one's way through a desperate or hopeless situation—gallows humor. That type of humor is not for everyone. I remember being diagnosed with a rather serious heart condition when I was twenty and titling my email updates things like "My Achy-Breaky Heart," much to my mother's dismay. I have a dark-humor bent, and she doesn't. That's okay.

But no matter your style, there are many different ways humor can be incorporated into your life. If you're like me, search for the funny angle, no matter the situation. If you're more like my mom, seek out humorous, lighthearted entertainment to lift your spirits. Give yourself permission to laugh at jokes, silly cat videos, and even your own goofs.

REFLECTION What's your humor style? Maybe when you do something embarrassing—like tripping spectacularly like I did the other day, in front of a large room of people—after a moment of hot embarrassment, you're able to pull out your phone to post about it on social media. Because if you can laugh about it with friends, it's not embarrassing anymore. Or maybe a silly show makes you giggle and realize we're all weird and awkward sometimes. How can you seek out the humor around you today?

MORNING ROUTINE

But I will sing of your strength, in the morning I will sing of your love; for you are my fortress, my refuge in times of trouble.

PSALM 59:16

Having a consistent, productive morning routine can have a huge impact on how the rest of your day feels. Your morning routine sets the tone.

Actually, that morning routine starts the night before, with going to bed on time so you can get up with your alarm, rather than fall out of bed five minutes before you have to rush out to catch the bus (not judging—that was me too).

Of course I'm going to tell you to eat a healthy, balanced breakfast, but how about a special playlist to listen to while you get ready? Something upbeat, full of songs you love. How about a few moments of silence to think only about God, instead of the many things you have to do today? What about a few self-care tasks? That can be anything from a warm shower to a few minutes playing with your dog. Anything that brings you joy is a good place to start.

REFLECTION Jot down your ideal morning routine. There are no wrong answers. Now figure out how much time that beautiful morning will take, then work backward to determine what time you need to get up and when you should go to sleep each night. Start tonight!

DAY 112

SING!

*I will sing to the LORD all my life; I will sing
praise to my God as long as I live.*

PSALM 104:33

There's something special about singing. Most people do it, even if we don't all sing particularly well. We might have a private concert in the shower, get into the music when we're alone in the car, or harmonize with our favorite song when we have our earbuds in and forget other people can hear us. (That's me.)

Singing—lifting praises to God—is mentioned so many times in Scripture, it's impossible to deny this is something we should be incorporating into our days. Singing, whether praise music or something else, has been studied in relation to mood and overall sense of well-being. Guess what the researchers found? Singing can help reduce stress. It has a positive impact on the happy chemicals in our brains and lowers our stress hormone levels. Amazing! God designed our bodies so beautifully.

So while I fully support singing absentmindedly in the shower or car or anywhere else, how about intentionally incorporating singing into your day? This habit will give you a nice little brain boost!

REFLECTION What are your favorite songs to belt? Do you have favorite worship songs you like to sing in church? Make a playlist designed especially for your new musical habit.

ROLE MODELS: HANNAH

> In her deep anguish Hannah prayed to the LORD, weeping
> bitterly. And she made a vow, saying, "LORD Almighty, if
> you will only look on your servant's misery and remember
> me, and not forget your servant but give her a son, then
> I will give him to the LORD for all the days of his life."
>
> **1 SAMUEL 1:10–11**

t's tempting to grow weary in prayer. Especially when it feels like our prayers have gone unanswered for ages. Maybe we decide the Lord is saying no. Sometimes he is, after all. But what about when we have an internal Holy Spirit nudge about something—that unshakeable sense we're supposed to keep asking?

We can imagine Hannah felt this nudge. She desperately wanted a child. She had prayed for years, and the Lord had not given her a child yet. That's where we are when Hannah makes this vow. She does get pregnant, and she keeps her promise to God. She dedicates her son to the temple when he's still a boy (how hard that must have been!). Her son grows up to be Samuel, one of Israel's greatest prophets and its final judge before the era of kings began.

If you're praying for something and you still feel prompted to keep asking, don't give up! The Lord hears you.

REFLECTION It takes wisdom to know when God says no to something, when it's a "No, not right now," or when we're supposed to keep asking in faith. Journaling out your prayers—and responses—can help sharpen that discernment over time. What can you journal out today?

ROLE MODELS: JOSHUA

> But if serving the LORD seems undesirable to you, then
> choose for yourselves this day whom you will serve [. . .]
> But as for me and my household, we will serve the LORD.
>
> **JOSHUA 24:15**

Starting with Exodus, Moses is definitely the star of the story for a while. The human star, anyway. We can learn a ton from Moses and how he became the man who led the Israelites, but sometimes his successor gets overlooked. Joshua actually led the Israelites into the promised land, as Moses had been barred from entering.

Joshua had been a faithful follower of God and assistant to Moses during the years the Israelites wandered in the desert. He displayed solid leadership as he took the Israelites into Canaan to settle where God had designated. Joshua is an example of determined, strong leadership. And here, his most famous quote: "As for me and my household, we will serve the LORD." (I'll bet you've seen that on a sign in someone's house.) Joshua knew how to take a stand for God.

REFLECTION It's a lot of responsibility to lead others. If you'd like to have leadership roles in the future, what qualities do you think you'll need? Read Joshua's story throughout Exodus (chapters 17, 24), Numbers (chapters 14, 27, 32), Deuteronomy (chapters 1, 3, 31, 34), and Joshua. Write down his best qualities, and think about how you could adapt them yourself.

MEETING TOGETHER

And let us consider how we may spur one another on toward
love and good deeds, not giving up meeting together, as some
are in the habit of doing, but encouraging one another—
and all the more as you see the Day approaching.

HEBREWS 10:24–25

Humans long for community. Even the reserved or introverted ones. Maybe community means a big group to you. Maybe it means one or two trusted close friends. But whatever the size, just about everyone wants other people who know them, understand them, and appreciate them. *Get* them.

Maybe this is one reason why the author of Hebrews encourages believers to continue to meet together. It's important to spend time with those who understand our faith. Who share it. Who understand what it means to "spur one another on toward love and good deeds." That has a specific meaning when you're a follower of Jesus.

That's why it's really important to make a habit of meeting together with other believers. For a lot of people, this happens Sunday mornings at church service. Some people also attend youth gatherings, special events, or Bible studies. Most churches, even small ones, have multiple opportunities for you to meet with fellow believers so everyone can meet how and when they're comfortable.

REFLECTION Have you been regularly meeting together with fellow believers lately? If not, what are the barriers you've faced? Brainstorm ways around those roadblocks.

THE STUDY OF SCRIPTURE

All Scripture is God-breathed and is useful for teaching, rebuking,
correcting and training in righteousness, so that the servant
of God may be thoroughly equipped for every good work.
2 TIMOTHY 3:16–17

Reading Scripture is really, really important. Books like this one are great. Bible studies are fantastic. Commentaries, when written by trusted sources, can definitely help us understand Scripture better. But just reading the Bible—the actual text—is incredibly important. Why?

Because without reading the actual Word of God, it's impossible to know if the external sources you're listening to are truthful to the whole of Scripture. That's a big task—trying to understand what's in the entire Bible and exactly what it's telling us. It's a task we're never really finished with—but the daily habit of reading the Bible is a wonderful way to start building up that knowledge base.

As we get more life experience, our understanding of Scripture grows, develops, and deepens. Think about it. You probably understood God a whole lot differently ten years, five years, maybe even one year ago than you do now. The more you study the Bible, the deeper your relationship with it becomes.

REFLECTION With Bible apps, it's easier than ever to read your Bible daily. You can use in-app reading plans and set reminders. If you prefer a physical Bible, great! Find a reading plan that looks doable for you. Many people like to read through the Bible each year, but don't be afraid to start small. Feel free to jot down the start of your plan here!

FIND POSITIVE FRIENDS

A friend loves at all times, and a brother
is born for a time of adversity.
PROVERBS 17:17

The Bible makes it clear that who we hang out with matters. Why is that part of our lives so important? Have you noticed how groups of friends who spend a lot of time together often rub off on each other? Sometimes there are so many inside jokes, they almost develop a language specific to that group. For example, I have one friend group where we send bagel GIFs to each other when we're about to meet up, and we don't explain why to anyone else.

Anyway, rubbing off on one another is a wonderful thing when you're hanging out with awesome people. It's less wonderful when you're hanging out with people who want to pull you away from your goals, your walk with Jesus, and the other good things in your life. I'm definitely not saying we should drop a friend who's going through a hard time in life or dealing with depression (not at all!). But we should also make an effort to spend time with people who understand the hopeful outlook we're shooting for and not spend as much time around people who don't share our overall aspirations.

REFLECTION Who are some of the optimistic, supportive people in your life? This list doesn't only have to be friends. Maybe your mom is a super sunny person who gives great advice. Maybe your siblings bring you joy. Make time to hang out with these positive influences in your life, whomever they are.

BE A POSITIVE FRIEND

May the God of hope fill you with all joy and peace
as you trust in him, so that you may overflow
with hope by the power of the Holy Spirit.

ROMANS 15:13

Remember that struggling friend we briefly mentioned in the last devotion? The one going through a time of grief or suffering from depression? As important as it is for you to hang out with uplifting, positive people, it's equally important for you to *be* the positive friend for someone else.

Being a positive presence in a struggling friend's life does not mean throwing your sunshine in that friend's face. That can quickly turn into the toxic positivity we talked about before. Instead, we should aim to be what the verse above describes—filled with joy and peace so we overflow with hope. If you expect to do this on your own power—and feel overwhelmed by that thought—I have good news for you. The Holy Spirit enables us to do this, not our own strength.

REFLECTION Is there a friend in your life who needs extra support right now? Think of how you can bring peace and joy into their presence without veering into toxic positivity. Can you offer a listening ear? Just be near them so they know they're not alone?

WE CAN'T EARN IT

For it is by grace you have been saved, through
faith—and this is not from yourselves, it is the gift of
God—not by works, so that no one can boast.

EPHESIANS 2:8–9

We've spent a lot of time talking about really good habits we can cultivate in our lives. And we've already learned focusing on the things we can control is helpful. But it's important to also remember one crucial truth: no matter how well we do in life, we can't earn our salvation by doing certain things or trying to control the outcome.

No amount of positive habit-building, good behavior, or optimism can earn salvation for us. This doesn't excuse us from good works—we're still called to do good in our own lives and the lives of others. But being a positive example in the world and living out our faith is fundamentally different from attempting to earn our standing with God.

As you make progress on your goals and habits, absolutely celebrate those wins. It's hard work. It takes consistency, self-control, and diligence. But always keep in mind you are a new creature and able to grow in Jesus's image because of *Christ's* work, not your own. And that is cause for celebration too!

REFLECTION When was the last time you thanked God for your salvation? That's another awesome habit to build—daily thanksgiving for what Christ has already done for us. Take a few moments to do that now, and let the joy of salvation fill you up again.

ROLE MODELS: MOSES

The LORD said to him, "Who gave human beings their mouths?
Who makes them deaf or mute? Who gives them sight or
makes them blind? Is it not I, the LORD? Now go; I will help
you speak and will teach you what to say." But Moses said,
"Pardon your servant, Lord. Please send someone else."

EXODUS 4:11-13

Remember our rock star from Exodus, Moses? This is how his life with the Lord began. God is trying to send him to Egypt to tell Pharaoh to let the Israelites go, as they were enslaved there at the time. Far from jumping at the opportunity to be the Lord's mouthpiece, Moses makes excuses, then simply says, "Please send someone else."

This is relatable. The Lord wasn't happy with Moses's refusal, but he granted his request to have someone else do the speaking (God chose Moses's brother, Aaron), while not letting Moses completely wiggle away from his calling. Then, Moses goes on to have a special relationship with God and leads the people of Israel for many years.

Moses started out afraid of the God-sized task before him. But the Lord grew him into his role, and he will grow us into ours!

REFLECTION Have you ever felt like God is calling you to something you're afraid to do? Or calling you to a role where you feel underequipped? You're in good company. Many of God's great prophets and leaders start out this way—afraid of their calling. You can say yes to God, even when you're afraid! Ask God to help you with the next steps you feel called to take.

SETTING LOVING LIMITS

Like a city whose walls are broken through
is a person who lacks self-control.
PROVERBS 25:28

The concept of boundaries has become popular in recent years, with good reason. When dealing with relationships and our own emotional lives, it's important to understand what boundaries are, as well as how we can utilize them in a godly way to enrich our relationships and set healthy standards.

The Bible tells us to exercise self-control, but our human nature often desires to control others. Boundaries define that dividing line. Boundaries say, "These things are my responsibility. These other things are your responsibility." In this way, we set loving limits on ourselves and others, only attempting to exert control over what's in our "yard" (the space within our boundary) and develop a clear idea of when someone is crossing the line into our yard. Boundaries help us know when to say no.

We will unpack specific examples over the next few days, but for now, just think about your boundary line as your property, containing all the things over which you have control—and responsibility.

REFLECTION Have you ever tried setting boundaries before? Can you think of some things that are definitely in your yard? Write a few of them down. (Your answers might vary from someone else's, but we all have some things in common: our own feelings are in our yard, for example.)

OWNING OUR THOUGHTS AND FEELINGS

Fools give full vent to their rage, but the wise bring calm in the end.
PROVERBS 29:11

Taking responsibility for our thoughts and feelings is *hard*. It just is. Many people struggle with this throughout their whole lives, be it always blaming others for how they feel, taking responsibility for others' emotions, or letting others' feelings heavily influence their own. And while it's true other people's behavior affects us, it's important to draw that distinction between their behavior and how we choose to respond. Their choices are in their yard; your choices are in your yard. Their feelings are in their yard; your feelings are in your yard.

When we recognize the way we respond—what we give space to in our minds—is something within our yard, that empowers us to exhibit the kind of self-control and wisdom the Bible talks about. We can separate our feelings from others' and create appropriate space between things that often feel far too entangled.

REFLECTION Do you tend to take responsibility for other people's feelings? Or perhaps you've just realized you have a hard time accepting responsibility for your own. No one is born with perfect boundaries. It takes practice! Think about the areas you have to grow in when it comes to boundary enforcement and boundary respect.

OWNING YOUR BODY

It is God's will that you should be sanctified: that you should avoid
sexual immorality; that each of you should learn to control your
own body in a way that is holy and honorable, not in passionate
lust like the pagans, who do not know God; and that in this matter
no one should wrong or take advantage of a brother or sister.

1 THESSALONIANS 4:3–6

This verse highlights our responsibility to respect our bodies—not
engaging in sexual immorality. And it highlights our responsibility
to respect others' boundaries—not wronging them in any way.

We use many words to draw these boundary lines. *Agency*: you
have power over what happens with your own body. *Consent*: no one
touches another person's body without their okay. *Autonomy*: each body
is independent of other bodies, and we must respect this distinction.

Bottom line: No one has the right to touch you if you don't want
them to. And you don't have the right to other people's bodies. Huggers
are awesome. But if the hugger is you, make sure you're respecting
others' boundaries *before* you touch them. It's important to honor and
respect both our own bodies and the bodies of others.

REFLECTION Body boundaries are more straightforward than other kinds
because our physical forms create clear dividing lines. It's evident something
is your body or not. And yet it's very common to have this boundary violated.
Take a moment to write down some of your healthy body boundaries and ways
you can communicate them with others.

OWNING OUR CHOICES

Do not be deceived: God cannot be mocked. A man reaps what he sows.

GALATIANS 6:7

The concept of reaping and sowing pops up a lot in Scripture. The basic idea is that you will experience the consequences of your actions, good or bad. It doesn't imply there's a cosmic tally of the good and bad everyone does and people are always rewarded or punished for what they've done. Each of us has seen good that seems to go unnoticed and wickedness that seems to go unpunished.

Instead, reaping and sowing is about the natural outpouring of our actions—and the spiritual consequences we may or may not see in the present moment. In other words, what we do has an effect on what happens around us. This principle is mentioned a lot, and still our human impulse is to blame others. Even from the very first sin (looking at you, Adam and Eve). We often try to justify ourselves. Do everything except take responsibility.

But part of having good boundaries is owning our choices, particularly our mistakes. We also need to recognize the positive impact of our actions, because that is important too!

REFLECTION You may have noticed it's a whole lot easier to own positive choices. It's definitely more comfortable than owning mistakes! But take a few moments to think about what you've been sowing this week. Are they seeds of righteousness? Of joy and peace? Or are they seeds of discord and conflict? Maybe something else entirely?

ROLE MODELS: PAUL

> Meanwhile, Saul was still breathing out murderous threats
> against the Lord's disciples. . . . As he neared Damascus
> on his journey, suddenly a light from heaven flashed
> around him. He fell to the ground and heard a voice say
> to him, "Saul, Saul, why do you persecute me?"
>
> **ACTS 9:1, 3-4**

A verse that begins with someone "breathing out murderous threats" doesn't sound like an obvious candidate for a biblical role model. But it is. Because this is the story of how Saul, persecutor of Christians, became the apostle Paul, and as much as any person in the New Testament, Paul's story shows us our pasts do not define us.

Saul met Jesus in a powerful, supernatural experience—it was probably the only way this man would become a follower of Christ. And unlike some other role models we look to when we talk about sketchy pasts, Saul was living according to the rules the religious leaders of his day applauded. He was a model citizen—the very best persecutor of these "rebels" against the faith. He is a testament to the fact we can be very wrong (while thinking we're right), repent of that wrongness, and be used powerfully for the kingdom. It starts with owning our mistakes.

REFLECTION Do you remember what it was like when you first met Jesus? Perhaps you have been going to church your whole life, and you can't remember *not* knowing about Jesus. Was there a time when he became more real for you? More personal?

ROLE MODELS: SAMSON

Samson said, "Let me die with the Philistines!" Then he
pushed with all his might, and down came the temple
on the rulers and all the people in it. Thus he killed
many more when he died than while he lived.

JUDGES 16:30

This is a brutal verse—and a tragic end to a life that ought to have been great. Samson is perhaps one of the most famous cautionary tales in the Bible. He began life with so much potential, born to parents who tried to help him uphold his Nazarite vow. He was Israel's judge, but Samson became entangled with a Philistine woman who didn't have his best interests at heart. He eventually told her the secret of his supernatural strength (his long hair was part of his vow and a symbol of his devotion to God), and when he decided to disobey God to please Delilah, it was the beginning of the end for Samson.

So why is he a role model? Because in his last act, he humbles himself and brings God-ordained judgment down on his Philistine captors, losing his life in the process. It's brutal but also inspiring. Samson proves that it's never too late. We can turn things around, choose God, choose righteousness, down to our last breath.

REFLECTION Samson's story is dramatic, but many people feel they've made mistakes God won't forgive them for. Do you have a friend who thinks God couldn't accept or love them? Maybe *you've* felt this way. Write a prayer—for yourself or for others who struggle with these false beliefs right now.

BUILDING A FENCE

Remind the people to be subject to rulers and authorities, to be obedient, to be ready to do whatever is good, to slander no one, to be peaceable and considerate, and always to be gentle toward everyone.

TITUS 3:1–2

We've been using a yard analogy when discussing boundaries—that the things in our yard are our responsibility. Can having a yard like this ever be a bad thing?

Yes—like everything good, boundaries can become bad if misused. Boundaries turn negative when we use them to build impenetrable walls to protect ourselves, excluding others and barricading our hearts. That's not a healthy use of boundaries, and it's not a good way to be ready to do "whatever is good," or "to be peaceable and considerate . . . gentle toward everyone."

Instead, think of your boundaries as a fence—a fence that has a gate. You can and should let people into your life, into your heart, and into your world. Remember, you have the right to close your gate to unhealthy expectations and things that will harm you or others.

REFLECTION When you visualize your boundary fence, imagining there's a gate you get to open and close, does it help you feel more empowered over your emotional life? Does it help you take responsibility for your thoughts and feelings while recognizing the negativity in your life that may be caused by others trying to barrel their way into your yard?

KIND REBUKE

"So watch yourselves. If your brother or sister sins against you, rebuke them; and if they repent, forgive them."

LUKE 17:3

Once we have created healthy boundaries, we might ask ourselves what happens when someone crosses a boundary. Because it will happen. People are imperfect, and even when they don't have bad intentions, boundary crossings are inevitable.

Jesus gives us some guidance in this verse. When our brother or sister sins against us, we are told to rebuke them. That means letting them know what boundary they've crossed—clearly, but also kindly, with words as gracious as possible. And we can let them know what we intend to do if our boundaries are crossed again. Perhaps it's distancing ourselves for a time. Maybe it requires speaking to someone else (especially appropriate if you need help dealing with an abusive situation).

Importantly, Jesus also tells us that if our brother or sister repents, we are to forgive them. Be sure to watch for true repentance—actions, not just words.

REFLECTION Dealing with confrontation is really hard for a lot of people. Is it hard for you? It's important to learn how to confront someone lovingly if you're going to maintain healthy boundaries. Take a few minutes to think through what you'll say and do when someone crosses the line.

REASSESSING BOUNDARIES

Bear with each other and forgive one another if any of you has
a grievance against someone. Forgive as the Lord forgave you.

COLOSSIANS 3:13

Here's a key piece to remember when thinking about your boundaries—it's important to reassess them often. Perhaps you needed very strong boundaries to protect yourself during a period of fragile mental health. Maybe you had to put intense boundaries around your time when you were under the wire on a huge end-of-semester project or your college applications or were busy with your starring role in the school play.

But the need for very strict boundaries is often seasonal, meaning when you're through that particular time in your life, you can take down that fence for a bit. And when it comes to restoring a relationship that's been broken, and it's one both parties want to restore, it's really important to keep watching for signs of repentance.

Remember, though—you can truly forgive a person without restoring the relationship with them. You can let go of offense and release all your anger and bitterness without reconnecting. Sometimes that's the best thing to do if a person is persisting in their sin against you or others.

REFLECTION Are there any circumstances in your life right now that call for strong "seasonal" boundaries? Or are you perhaps coming out of a season like that, and it's time to reassess your boundaries and open the gate more freely?

ROLE MODELS: JOSEPH

But Joseph said to them, "Don't be afraid. Am I in the place of
God? You intended to harm me, but God intended it for good
to accomplish what is now being done, the saving of many
lives. So then, don't be afraid. I will provide for you and your
children." And he reassured them and spoke kindly to them.

GENESIS 50:19–21

Poor Joseph. Despite his status as the favored child in his family, he really went through it. First his brothers attacked him. Then they sold him into slavery. Then his master's wife tried to accuse him of assault—when in fact she'd been the one to try to start something with him. Despite all this, God was with him. Joseph ended up in an Egyptian prison, but even then, he rose to a place of prominence, and then he was well positioned to rescue his family, who would become patriarchs of the twelve tribes of Israel.

Joseph's life shows us that sometimes God's big plans involve personal hardships that bring about a greater good. But it also shows us an example of strength in the face of people trying to pull us down. So much of what happened to Joseph was because of others' unhealthiness—they were jealous or lustful. But Joseph refused to be defined by their choices, and God used him in a powerful, important way.

REFLECTION Has something difficult ever happened to you that you later realized resulted in a better outcome than you could have imagined? These things aren't particularly common, but when they happen, it's really clear that God is moving!

GROWING IN GRATITUDE

Enter his gates with thanksgiving and his courts with
praise; give thanks to him and praise his name.
PSALM 100:4

When there's a lot happening around us that's negative, it's easy to get sucked into the whirlwind of that negativity. And when we do, sometimes we forget the many things we have to be grateful for.

Gratitude doesn't erase hard things we're dealing with. It's not helpful or healthy to ignore our grief by telling ourselves we shouldn't feel the way we do because we have [fill-in-the-blank blessings]. But it *is* helpful to remember we can choose to focus on our blessings instead of our hardships. And, when we're not going through a season of hardship, it's definitely appropriate to overflow with gratitude.

Spend today (or the whole week!) intentionally choosing gratitude. As you move through your day, take note of all the blessings, large and small, you come across. You might be surprised at how much God has given to you that you never even noticed before.

REFLECTION Try the experiment above using a gratitude journal. Jot down everything you notice, and maybe even spend some extra time in prayer about what you wrote, thanking God for his goodness. How many of those blessings were things you regularly thank God for? How many were things you hadn't noticed before?

THE BLESSINGS OF FAMILY AND HOME

Honor your father and your mother, as the LORD your God has commanded you, so that you may live long and that it may go well with you in the land the LORD your God is giving you.

DEUTERONOMY 5:16

Families come in all shapes and sizes. So do homes. But if you have people who love you taking care of you and a roof over your head—a place to call home—you are blessed! We may take these things for granted sometimes, but truly, family and home are two of life's greatest blessings.

Perhaps your home situation isn't particularly stable. If so, you're not alone. Many people experience difficult family life growing up, and housing insecurity is a huge problem around the world. If we're in one or both of these situations, sometimes we experience the blessings of family and home in slightly less obvious ways—friends who are like family, and the provision of shelter even if it's not in the form of a house or apartment. We can also be mindful of these blessings, even when they take less traditional forms.

REFLECTION If you have never had an unstable family situation or housing insecurity, that's wonderful! But many people are experiencing those very things right now. How can you get involved in your local community to help bring the blessings of family and home to others? And if you are experiencing instability, talk to God about what you're going through.

DAY 133

ROLE MODELS: JOHN THE APOSTLE

One of them, the disciple whom Jesus loved, was reclining next to him.
JOHN 13:23

Like with the name Mary, there are a lot of Johns in the New Testament. This John is the author of the Gospel of John, and he is traditionally seen as being one of Jesus's twelve disciples.

Throughout his gospel, John referred to himself as "the disciple whom Jesus loved" or in similar phrases. When Jesus would pull a small group from the twelve disciples, John was selected. Even Jesus had best friends.

Close friends—heart friends—are very important. It's vital to have people who get us. Who love us. Who care about us enough to tell us the hard truth when we need to hear it. Proverbs 27:6 reminds us, "Wounds from a friend can be trusted, but an enemy multiplies kisses." We can imagine heart friends were a little different for Jesus, and still he had those he especially clicked with—those he wanted in his inner circle. In fact, he even trusted John to take care of his mom, Mary.

REFLECTION Think about your heart friends. Maybe you have one or two, or maybe you have several. What is something you can do this week to let your heart friends know how appreciated they are?

THE BLESSING OF ENJOYMENT

I know that there is nothing better for people than to be happy and to do good while they live. That each of them may eat and drink, and find satisfaction in all their toil—this is the gift of God.

ECCLESIASTES 3:12–13

Have you ever been doing something you really enjoy and just stopped to think, "Wow. I really love this"? Or maybe you've even experienced a sense of joy while doing the most mundane tasks—like putting clothes away or doing dishes alongside a favorite relative after a meal. The fact we are able to feel happiness as we learn, play, explore, rest, work, and grow is a tremendous blessing.

Sometimes we associate the idea of pleasure with sinfulness or excess, but they're not necessarily connected. When we make a point to take pleasure in the small joys of life, it's actually part of the godly practice of gratitude.

Thanking God for the big answer to prayer—an excellent grade on the test you were worried about, the winning goal at your soccer game, the college acceptance letter you were hoping for—seems obvious. But how often do we thank God for the little things—how good it feels to drink a glass of water when you're thirsty, the way the springtime sunshine feels on your skin, or finding the perfect pack of multicolor pens (don't judge me!).

REFLECTION Without thinking too hard, quickly write down everything you can think of that you enjoy, from the big to the smallest of the small. Give yourself a set amount of time to do this—maybe five minutes—and see how many things you can come up with.

THE BLESSINGS OF SALVATION AND SANCTIFICATION

You were washed, you were sanctified, you were justified in the
name of the Lord Jesus Christ and by the Spirit of our God.

1 CORINTHIANS 6:11

Salvation is probably pretty high on the gratitude list for most follow-ers of Jesus. The Son of God literally became a man, lived a sinless life, died on the cross to reconcile us to God, and we now get to spend eternity with him. That's a really huge blessing. In fact, it's the biggest blessing we could possibly imagine, and no matter what else is going on in our lives, we can always be assured of our salvation.

But we might overlook a related blessing—our sanctification. Once we are saved, God doesn't leave us in our brand-new, baby Christian state for long. He immediately begins shaping us in his image, molding our character to look more like Jesus's. The Holy Spirit dwells inside us to help us in this process—he convicts us, then enables us to grow in godliness as we mature in our faith.

Becoming like Jesus isn't easy, and it isn't always fun. But when we look back to see our growth and how much progress we've made, it's immensely gratifying.

REFLECTION Do you remember what life was like—what *you* were like—before you accepted Jesus and God's grace? Do you recall what your character was like in the early stages of your sanctification? How does it compare to now, a little farther along in your spiritual journey?

ROLE MODELS: ESTHER

"For if you remain silent at this time, relief and deliverance
for the Jews will arise from another place, but you and your
father's family will perish. And who knows but that you have
come to your royal position for such a time as this?"

ESTHER 4:14

The book of Esther is famous for being one of the two books of the Bible that never mention God (the other is Song of Songs). And yet, though he's not mentioned by name, his presence is clearly felt. Esther is a book about the preservation of God's people.

Esther was a young Jewish woman living during the Exilic Period—the time after Babylon conquered Jerusalem, and Persia then conquered Babylon. She is put in a position where she is able to speak to the Persian king on behalf of her people—something she's a little reluctant about. The Jews were being persecuted, and though it was probably terrifying and there were a lot of risks, Esther spoke up for them so they would not be killed.

Esther is a role model we can look toward whenever we feel afraid to do what we know is right. She's a role model who can encourage us when we want to speak up for the oppressed. And she's a role model we can remember when we get the sense we're stepping into a role we were born for.

REFLECTION Do you sometimes find it difficult to be courageous? Most of us do. How do you react when you don't feel brave enough to step up? Brainstorm some ways you can bolster your courage the next time you need to be brave.

ROLE MODELS: JOHN THE BAPTIST

Then Jesus came from Galilee to the Jordan to be baptized
by John. But John tried to deter him, saying, "I need
to be baptized by you, and do you come to me?"
MATTHEW 3:13-14

John the Baptist spent a number of years fulfilling his role as Jesus's
forerunner—the one who would proclaim the coming of God's Son.
He was a wandering preacher, traveling from place to place to preach
repentance and the need for a new beginning through baptism. He had
many followers, and even now he is regarded as a prophet, a holy man,
an important religious figure.

You could say John the Baptist was pretty good at the task set
before him. But when Jesus began his earthly ministry, John was hes-
itant to baptize Jesus, instead recognizing Jesus should be baptizing
him. Despite his status as a faithful prophet, John had the humility to
recognize Jesus was greater than him—even though it wouldn't be too
far-fetched to imagine they could have been rivals.

But John did not see himself as better or more knowledgeable. He
baptized Jesus at his insistence, and the rest is history.

REFLECTION Our culture doesn't always value or cultivate humility. This
is unfortunate! Can you think of some positive, healthy traits that arise from a
humble heart? (One that comes to mind for me: the ability to admit you were
wrong about something.)

SCIENTIFICALLY PROVEN: EXERCISE AND SLEEP

Dear friend, I pray that you may enjoy good health and that all may go well with you, even as your soul is getting along well.

3 JOHN 1:2

We've pulled a lot of wisdom from the Bible, looked at who God is, and checked out a bunch of role models from Scripture. But have you wondered what science has to say about positivity and cultivating an optimistic outlook? Would it surprise you if it supports what the Bible tells us?

Our bodies were made to move, and a bunch of processes occur in them when we get active, including the release of hormones that help improve mood. But if you think that means you have to live at the gym, think again. Just seven minutes of activity per day is enough to reap the mood-boosting benefits.

Unsurprisingly, sleep is also scientifically proven to have a big impact on our happiness. When we get enough hours of quality sleep, we are less sensitive to the impact of negative emotions. Life feels more manageable and our problems like obstacles we can overcome, rather than roadblocks stopping us in our tracks. Looking after our physical needs is good for both our body health *and* our mental well-being.

REFLECTION Have you been working on activity- and sleep-related goals lately? If so, what has your progress been like so far? If you haven't started yet, what are some actions you could take today? Remember, small steps toward a larger goal will give you forward momentum.

SCIENTIFICALLY PROVEN: HUMAN CONNECTION

As iron sharpens iron, so one person sharpens another.
PROVERBS 27:17

Research shows that people who feel connected to their friends and family report greater levels of happiness. People really matter to us, and this should come as no surprise. God created people for himself but also for each other. He put us in communities—cultures, family groups, neighborhoods, and churches (meaning groups of people worshiping together, not the buildings). Having a strong sense of community promotes stability, wellness, and happiness.

You know what else helps us feel happier long-term? Helping others. Serving people in need adds a layer of meaning to our lives, helping combat feelings of helplessness or uselessness that can sometimes be overwhelming. Research shows that about one hundred hours of service per year is the point you might notice an impact on your emotional well-being. But anything you can do helps!

REFLECTION One hundred hours of service per year works out to a little over eight hours per month. Is there some volunteer work you can do that will add up to this amount? Revisit what you wrote down during our devotions about serving others to help spark more ideas.

SCIENTIFICALLY PROVEN: FRESH AIR AND SMILES

Let everything that has breath praise the LORD. Praise the LORD.

PSALM 150:6

God created a big, beautiful world, and it should come as no surprise that science proves we should get out there and enjoy it—even if it's only your tiny corner of the world. Breathing fresh air outside for twenty minutes per day has been shown to increase happiness. Think you have to wait until summertime to do this? Nope! Scientists studied optimal temperatures and found that 57 degrees had the greatest positive impact on mood. Seriously!

While you're outside breathing fresh air, be sure to smile at those who pass you. Research shows that smiling—true smiles that reach all the way up to our eyes—actually make us happier. Perhaps it's the muscles we're moving that trigger this response. Maybe it's making a connection with someone else, even if it's only for a moment. Whatever it is, it's an easy and great way to lift our spirits, and the spirits of people around us!

REFLECTION If you lead a busy life filled with school and activities and volunteer work and social time, it can be hard to think about adding one more thing. But taking a break outside for twenty minutes to breathe fresh air is worth it! How can you incorporate this today?

SCIENTIFICALLY PROVEN: PLAN A TRIP

In their hearts humans plan their course, but
the LORD establishes their steps.

PROVERBS 16:9

As followers of Christ, we recognize our ultimate outcomes aren't in our hands. We recognize God ordains our steps. However, the Bible clearly supports thinking about—and planning for—the future wisely (see the parable of the bags of gold in Matthew 25:14–30).

Science also backs up the idea that planning for the future is good for us. Specifically, planning a trip. Things like choosing a place to go, thinking about how you'll get there, deciding what you'd like to see, investigating local cuisine you'd like to try. And, if possible, beginning to set aside some funds to make the trip happen. But do you want to know something cool? Even if you never take the trip, just the act of *planning* it increases happiness and boosts your mood.

Why? Scientists theorize that looking ahead to something good keeps your focus on the future, rather than the hardships or boredom of today. It's a fun, long-term goal to think about and work toward.

REFLECTION   Maybe the idea of planning a trip for yourself seems crazy right now (depending on your age, we could be talking about ten or more years away!), but it's never too soon to start dreaming. Where would you go? Make a top ten list of places you'd like to visit, then enjoy the process of either narrowing it down or continuing to add to it.

SCIENTIFICALLY PROVEN: MEDITATION AND GRATITUDE

Within your temple, O God, we meditate on your unfailing
love. Like your name, O God, your praise reaches to the ends
of the earth; your right hand is filled with righteousness.

PSALM 48:9–10

Sometimes Christians react negatively to the word *meditate*, but the Bible talks about meditating a lot. For Christians, meditating means clearing the static of daily life from our minds to focus on studying the Word of God. When we intentionally and thoughtfully focus on Scripture like this, it opens us to God's presence and an overwhelming sense of peace and gratitude.

And speaking of gratitude, research shows that people who make a point to focus on gratitude are happier and report higher levels of satisfaction in their lives. The icing on top of living a grateful life is sharing that gratitude with others. If there's someone who has helped, supported, or encouraged you lately, tell them how much you appreciate them.

REFLECTION Keeping a gratitude journal helps the practice of growing in gratitude, tracking specific things you're grateful for. Try it now in the space below. What are you grateful for today? What are some things you're always grateful for? Pick one of these things, and use that in your meditation time today, focusing on your thankfulness to God.

SCIENTIFICALLY PROVEN: GETTING OLDER

Gray hair is a crown of splendor; it is attained in the way of righteousness.

PROVERBS 16:31

Research shows that getting older increases happiness. Wait, *what*? In our youth-obsessed culture, people report getting *happier* as they grow older?

Yep, that's right. There are a lot of theories as to why this may be. Perhaps older people appreciate that they're still hanging in there. Or they've let go of things that used to seem so important—dressing a certain way, achieving certain things, acquiring certain stuff. Or maybe they have shifted their priorities to things that feel more enjoyable, more peaceful, or more meaningful.

Whatever the reason, this finding is supported by Scriptural wisdom. The Bible has always called it a blessing to live to old age, have grandchildren, and be old enough to watch your hair turn gray. Long life is not granted to everyone—if you're lucky enough to experience it, enjoy it! And it never hurts to start enjoying every day you have now.

REFLECTION Have you ever thought about getting older as a blessing? What can you do to start "living like an older person" now? Hint: What things *feel* important but aren't actually meaningful in your life? Can you refocus your priorities on the things that really matter?

JESUS HAS OVERCOME

*"I have told you these things, so that in me you
may have peace. In this world you will have trouble.
But take heart! I have overcome the world."*

JOHN 16:33

I have overcome the world" are some of the most encouraging words in
the entire Bible. Before saying this, Jesus had just finished describing
some really hard things: The disciples would be scattered. They would
abandon him. Jesus would leave for a time (though he did promise to
return). But then he says he told them these things so they would have
peace. The world brings trouble, but take heart! He has overcome.

Troubles will come for us too. The world is not getting less dark
or difficult. But we do not need to panic about this or, worse, infer that
God has abandoned us. We do not need to be dismayed by life's troubles,
even when we find them painful (and remember—it's okay to acknowledge when something hurts). Through it all, we have the peace and
assurance that comes with knowing the very end of the story. Christ
returns, victorious.

REFLECTION How does your perspective shift when you think about Jesus
having overcome the world? Death itself was defeated on the cross. We know
the ending of the story!

GOD KNOWS OUR ANXIETIES

I sought the LORD, and he answered me; he
delivered me from all my fears.

PSALM 34:4

Sometimes people are miraculously and instantly cured of their anxiety. Other times, genuine, faithful Christians battle their anxiety on an ongoing basis. Perhaps it's the thorn in their side—the thing they pray about, asking God to remove it for them, and he chooses not to (if the apostle Paul had a thorn, we sure can too—see 2 Corinthians 12:7–10).

But one thing each and every one of us can feel absolutely assured of: God knows about our anxiety. He *sees* it. He cares about it. Pain, fear, illness—no one likes to experience these things, but we know we have a God who sees and comforts us in our affliction, whatever it is.

This is a great source of encouragement for any Christian walking through this life, looking forward to the next, working to become more like Jesus each passing day. Be encouraged, friend. He understands your heart.

REFLECTION   Sometimes when we speak to God, we feel like we must be on our "best behavior." And while a sense of reverence and respect is definitely appropriate, we don't need to hold back our real feelings or struggles from God. He already knows them! Can you pray in a raw, honest way right now?

GOD IS WORKING OUT HIS PLAN

And we know that in all things God works for the good of those who love him, who have been called according to his purpose.

ROMANS 8:28

We spent time developing a better understanding of God's character—his traits and what each of those traits looks like in a holy God (often quite different from how they look in sinful humans). Why did we do that?

Because only when we understand who God really is, what his character is all about, can we fully appreciate verses like this. God is working out his big-picture plan in the world, his plan for his people, and his plan in our lives. And those plans will ultimately be good for us. Because our all-knowing, ever-present, all-powerful, perfectly good, purely holy, mercifully just, eternal God is always operating within his character.

Hear this promise, friend—God is working *all things* for the good of those who love him. That's you. That's me. Sometimes we'll face others wanting to tear us down or circumstances that are legitimately difficult (even terrible!). But God is with us, always working for our good.

REFLECTION What's one of God's attributes you've seen on display in your life this week? Maybe his goodness was revealed in a special little blessing only he would know you desired. Maybe his mercy was evident when you confessed something and felt deep peace afterward.

WE DON'T HAVE TO HAVE IT FIGURED OUT

Trust in the LORD with all your heart and lean not on
your own understanding; in all your ways submit
to him, and he will make your paths straight.

PROVERBS 3:5–6

Want to know a secret, friend? You don't have to have it all figured out. Wait, what? We've been talking about all these things you can do, little steps and big steps to take to help shape your outlook on life. To help you stay positive in the midst of a very trying world.

These things are certainly helpful. Hopefully you feel like your positivity toolbox is full of useful ideas that will allow you to make progress in lots of areas of your life. And yet, it is not only okay, it's *necessary* to acknowledge we don't have it all figured out. God wants us to try our very best—to do good works in his name, to be reflections of Jesus shining in this broken world—but we are limited. Small. Imperfect.

And that's freeing. Because it means God doesn't expect us to *be* him. He simply expects us to *trust* him.

REFLECTION Imagine breathing in all your worries, as well as your plans and goals and dreams. Hold that breath, that heavy weight, in your lungs for a few seconds. Now release the breath and imagine handing control over to God. Write down those cares, whether they're unhealthy anxieties or healthy plans, and give them over to God. Put them in his wise, powerful hands.

GOD FORGIVES US

> "If my people, who are called by my name, will humble
> themselves and pray and seek my face and turn from
> their wicked ways, then I will hear from heaven, and
> I will forgive their sin and will heal their land."

2 CHRONICLES 7:14

A lot of things can contribute to a dark outlook on life. From physical factors, like brain chemistry, to emotional factors, like dealing with past trauma, those struggling with positivity generally have a complex set of influences making this extra difficult for them.

But sometimes sin is part of that complex web. Now, hear me out. I am *not* suggesting we be like Job's friends in Job 4–23 or the disciples asking Jesus about the blind man, who said, "Who sinned, this man or his parents, that he was born blind?" (John 9:2). I am suggesting we search our *own* hearts on this matter, not condemn ourselves. And because God is merciful and loving, if we have unconfessed sin in our lives, he wants us to repent, and when we do so he is quick to forgive.

Remember, God doesn't leave us stuck. We are equipped with the Holy Spirit to help us overcome. We have friends or family to help hold us accountable. We have Scripture to encourage and correct us.

REFLECTION Whether it's a contributing factor to your outlook on life or not, we know everyone sins. Have you asked God lately to reveal any areas of sin you might not be aware of? It's a good idea to do that periodically, because sometimes our sins become habits we don't even notice anymore.

GOD HELPS US

"For I am the LORD your God who takes hold of your right
hand and says to you, Do not fear; I will help you."

ISAIAH 41:13

The idea of trying to live like Jesus is a bit overwhelming. How can we possibly do so much good, love people so well, stay so connected to the Father?

The answer is we can't—not as well as Jesus did, anyway! But the process of trying is why we're here. And we're in luck. God doesn't command us to do things and then walk away. He's *here* with us. Helping us. It's easy to read the Old Testament and feel a little envious that the Israelites had the presence of God literally appearing before them, guiding them, speaking to them, rebuking them (okay, maybe we're not envious of that part . . .).

And the Israelites had a very special thing. But we have the Holy Spirit now. We have the guide, the comforter, the one who convicts, living in our hearts. God is as present with us as he was with the Israelites, and he's here to help us on our journeys.

REFLECTION Is there something that feels overwhelming or impossible in your life right now? Spend some time in prayer, asking the Holy Spirit for guidance—or even simply for peace and comfort.

GOD RENEWS

> "'He will wipe every tear from their eyes. There will
> be no more death' or mourning or crying or pain,
> for the old order of things has passed away."
>
> **REVELATION 21:4**

God is making all things new. When Jesus returns, the world will be reborn. New Earth will reflect what the Lord originally intended—a perfect world, unharmed by sin. No death, no pain, no suffering.

While we wait, there's good news. God is making things new in this very moment. While we wait, God is renewing hearts. He is awakening souls, he is *changing* things in real and powerful ways.

He is renewing you, friend. There is no past so bad God cannot redeem it. There is no sin so big God cannot forgive it. There is no mind so hopeless, no heart so broken, that God cannot renew it. And there is no circumstance so overwhelming that God can't help you through in some way. God is in the habit of giving new life to those thought to be dead. God restores, and to him be the glory forever and ever.

REFLECTION Let's end our journey together by praying Psalm 51:10–12: "Create in me a pure heart, O God, and renew a steadfast spirit within me. Do not cast me from your presence or take your Holy Spirit from me. Restore to me the joy of your salvation and grant me a willing spirit, to sustain me."

How does that make you feel going forward?

"Positive Thinking: Stop Negative Self-Talk to Reduce Stress."
Mayo Clinic Staff. Stress Management, Mayo Clinic, February 3,
2022; https://www.mayoclinic.org/healthy-lifestyle/stress
-management/in-depth/positive-thinking/art-20043950.

"Optimism and Your Health." Harvard Health Publishing, Harvard
University, May 1, 2008; https://www.health.harvard.edu/heart
-health/optimism-and-your-health.

"Benefits of Positive Thinking for Body and Mind." Kendra Cherry,
medically reviewed by David Susman, PhD. Verywell Mind,
updated June 1, 2020; https://www.verywellmind.com/benefits
-of-positive-thinking-2794767.

"The Power of Positive Thinking." Johns Hopkins Medicine, Health,
accessed July 5, 2022; https://www.hopkinsmedicine.org/health
/wellness-and-prevention/the-power-of-positive-thinking.

"Benefits of Thinking Positively, and How to Do It." Adrianne Santos-
Longhurst, medically reviewed by Timothy J. Legg, PhD, PsyD.
Healthline, February 21, 2019; https://www.healthline.com
/health/how-to-think-positive#summary.

"How to Be More Optimistic." Susan Shain. *New York Times,* February
18, 2020, updated March 23, 2020; https://www.nytimes.com
/2020/02/18/smarter-living/how-to-be-more-optimistic.html.

"Using Learned Optimism in Your Life." Kendra Cherry, medically
reviewed by Rachel Goldman, PhD, FTOS. Verywell Mind,
June 28, 2021; https://www.verywellmind.com/learned-
optimism-4174101.

"How to Be More Optimistic." Hannah Hollingsworth, medically
reviewed by Melinda Ratini, DO, MS. WebMD.com, September 9,
2021; https://www.webmd.com/balance/features/more-optimistic.

"Should We Always Look for Silver Linings?" Kira M. Newman. *Greater Good Magazine,* Greater Good Science Center, December 13, 2016; https://greatergood.berkeley.edu/article/item/should_we _always_look_for_silver_linings.

"The Discovery of Bacteria." Aria Nouri, MD. American Association for the Advancement of Science, Scientia blog post, July 5, 2011; https://www.aaas.org/discovery-bacteria.

"10 Ways that Singing Benefits Your Health." Rebecca Joy Stanborough, medically reviewed by Debra Rose Wilson, PhD, MSN, RN, IBCLC, AHN-BC, CHT. Healthline, November 10, 2020; https://www .healthline.com/health/benefits-of-singing.

"Low-Stress and High-Stress Singing Have Contrasting Effects on Glucocorticoid Response." Daisy Fancourt, Lisa Aufegger, Aaron Willamon. Centre for Performance Science, Royal College of Music, London, UK, *Front. Psychol.,* Sec. Performance Science, September 4, 2015; https://doi.org/10.3389/fpsyg.2015.01242.

"10 Scientifically Proven Ways to Be Incredibly Happy." Jeff Haden. *Inc.*, accessed July 6, 2022; https://www.inc.com/jeff-haden/10 -scientifically-proven-ways-to-be-incredibly-happy-wed.html.

"Old People Are Happier than People in Their 20s." Mandy Oaklander. *TIME,* accessed online July 6, 2022; https://time.com/collection /guide-to-happiness/4464811/aging-happiness-stress-anxiety -depression/.

"Paradoxical Trend for Improvement in Mental Health With Aging: A Community-Based Study of 1,546 Adults Aged 21–100 Years." Michael L. Thomas, PhD, et al. *The Journal of Clinical Psychiatry*, August 2016, 77(8):e1019-25; https://www.psychiatrist.com/jcp /mental/improvement-in-mental-health-with-aging/.

"The Aging Paradox: The Older We Get, the Happier We Are." Deborah Netburn. *Los Angeles Times,* August 24, 2016; https://www .latimes.com/science/sciencenow/la-sci-sn-older-people-happier -20160824-snap-story.html.

"The Mental Health Benefits of Learning a New Skill." Alison Rodericks. *Upskilled*, accessed July 6, 2022; https://www.upskilled .edu.au/skillstalk/mental-health-benefits-learning-new-skill.

"The Mind-Body Benefits of Learning a New Skill." Piedmont Healthcare website, accessed July 6, 2022; https://www.piedmont .org/living-better/the-mind-body-benefits-of-learning-a-new-skill.

"The Many Benefits of Lifelong Learning." Walden University website, accessed July 6, 2022; https://www.waldenu.edu/programs /resource/the-many-benefits-of-lifelong-learning.

Adored

In an ever-changing world, we can be certain of one thing: we are beloved by God. *Adored: 365 Devotions for Young Women* tackles tough topics you face, from bullying and social media to friendships and dating, while also helping you see how infinitely precious you are in God's sight.

Beloved

Relationships. Body image. Peer pressure. Chasing your dreams. These are just a few of the topics explored in *Beloved: 365 Devotions for Young Women,* with daily readings to help you navigate the things that matter most in life.

Available wherever books are sold!

A Mindful Moment

This 150-day devotional focuses on four key categories—physical sensations, negative emotions, compassion to self, and lovingkindness to others. It can be used as a guide for daily meditation and reflection but allows for flexibility, providing inspiration and God's peace in any situation. Use it on your journey to self-love and then let it take you to a place of love for all as Jesus calls us to love.

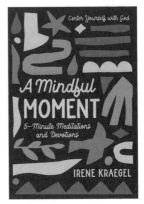

A Mindful Moment includes:

- A how-to guide to simple meditation

- A brief history of Christian meditation practices

- A simple yet inspirational design that makes is perfect for anyone in need of time with God

- 150 Scripturally based devotions which include a Bible verse, a short but significant reflection, and a suggested meditation practice such as cradling the breath, hearing meditation, or letting go of thought

Available wherever books are sold!